THE REMARKABLE HUNTINGTONS

✣

ARCHER AND ANNA

Mary Mitchell

The Remarkable Huntingtons

Archer and Anna

Chronicle of a Marriage

by

MARY MITCHELL
ALBERT GOODRICH

edited by
Andrea Zimmermann

BUDD DRIVE PRESS
NEWTOWN, CONNECTICUT
2004

FRONTISPIECE: Archer and Anna Huntington with pets at Rocas, 1935. Anna Hyatt Huntington Papers, Syracuse University Library, Special Collections Research Center.

ENDPAPERS: A portion of the wall at the Mariners' Museum. The brick is laid up in the pattern called "Huntington Squeeze."

Published by The Budd Drive Press
P.O. Box 309, Newtown, CT 06470

Although the authors have made every effort to ensure the accuracy and completeness of information contained in this book, we assume no responsibility for errors, inaccuracies, omissions, or any inconsistency herein. Any slights of people, places or organizations are unintentional.

FIRST PRINTING 2004

Library of Congress Control Number: 2004091082
Mitchell, Mary 1912–
Goodrich, Albert 1920–2004
The Remarkable Huntingtons, Archer and Anna, Chronicle of a Marriage
by Mary Mitchell and Albert Goodrich.
pages: 168
illustrations: 63
Includes bibliography and index.

ISBN 0-9749644-0-9

1. Huntington, Archer Milton, capitalist, philanthropist, poet, bibliophile, 1870–1955
2. Huntington, Anna Hyatt, sculptor, farmer, housewife, 1876–1973
Both in the United States of America

Profits from the sale of this book will be divided two ways. One-half will go to the Lt. James A. Goodrich Memorial Scholarship Fund at the Newtown High School, Newtown, Connecticut 06470. The other half will go to the Hispanic Society of America, 613 West 155th Street, New York, N.Y. 10032.

Credits: Every effort has been made to identify copyright holders of illustrations or portions of text; in case of oversight and on notification to the publisher, corrections will be made in the next edition.

PRINTED IN THE UNITED STATES OF AMERICA

To the memory of
ARCHER AND ANNA HUNTINGTON
who captured our interest and affection as,
while reading Anna's diaries, we watched their lives unfold,
lives infused with mutual respect and pleasure
in caring for each other.

TABLE OF CONTENTS

ACKNOWLEDGMENTS

WE EXTEND OUR WARM THANKS for the advice, help, and material furnished by many people interested in our book, and are particularly grateful:

To the Department of Special Collections at the Syracuse University E. S. Bird Library for the use of the *Anna Hyatt Huntington Papers* and the *Archer Milton Huntington Papers*; and to Kathleen Manwaring, Carolyn Davis and Diane Cooter, archivists, who had seventeen of Anna's diaries photocopied and sent to us.

To Ann Marshall, independent researcher, who did research for us when we could not go to Syracuse. She found the Stanerigg house-plans, information about the farm, and articles about deerhounds and how Stanerigg Kennels was run.

To the Hispanic Society of America and to Dr. Gerald J. MacDonald, Librarian, to Susan Rosenstein, Curator of Manscripts, Costancia del Alamo, Curator of Sculptures, Diane Liddy, Rights and Reproductions, and Camila Olaso, President of the Friends of the H.S.A. and Coordinator of Development and Public Relations for the Society. Each gave us unremitting help in answering all manner of questions.

To Susan Harris Edwards and the University of South Carolina for permitting us to extract material from her Master's thesis: "*Anna Hyatt Huntington: Sculptor and Patron of American Idealism.*" Her scholarly thesis gave us valuable insights into Anna's work and a useful chronology of her life and her sculpture.

To the reference librarians of the C. H. Booth Library in Newtown, Connecticut, Beryl Harrison, Mary Antey, and Jocelyn Bagger. A great deal of our information came from books obtained through Inter-Library Loan, an incomparable service.

To John McDonnell, reference librarian of Danbury Public Library, who found us a copy of Doris E. Cook's monograph about Anna Hyatt Huntington.

To the reference librarians of the Mark Twain Library in Redding, Connecticut, which has an abundant file of Huntington material.

To Beth Paul, reference librarian at the Westport Public Library, who found the interview with Cesare Contini, plaster caster, in the *Archives of American Art* at the Smithsonian Institution, an important part of our chapter on Anna and her sculpture.

To Dr. Dan Lewis, Curator of American Historical Manuscripts, of The Huntington Library, Art Collections, and Botanical Gardens, San Marino, California. Dan kindly answered Mary's many questions about Archer and his family ties on the west coast.

To residents of Redding, Connecticut, who helped us: Henry Rasmussen, caretaker of Stanerigg Farm 1955–1973; Mrs. Thomas Lalley, Anna's secretary during WWII; Mrs. Margaret Wixsted, Redding historian.

To Edith Szatai, friend and linguist, who started us off with translating the chapter of *El Poeta y La*

Escultora by José García-Mazas that described how Archer and Anna first met.

To Jane Buitron and Teresa Carmona, independent researchers, who translated portions of *El Poeta y La Escultora*, biography of Archer, written by José García-Mazas.

To Anna's relatives: her nephew, Alfred Mayor who identified the people in the 1948 Christmas family photograph; Martha Mayor Smith, Yeardley Smith, and Sandra Cook, daughter of Ridgely Cook, Harriet Mayor's grandson. Sandra led us to other members of the Hyatt and Mayor families.

To Lucia Nebel White, Berthold Nebel's daughter, who as Anna's friend and photographer visited Stanerigg often and shared with us her memories of Stanerigg's interior rooms and the Huntingtons' life there. Lucia took us to the National Academy of Design.

To Dorcas MacClintock, sculptor, who led us to our sculpture consultant.

To Elisabeth Gordon Chandler, friend and adviser, who critiqued our chapter on Anna and her sculpture. Her help was invaluable. As a young sculptor, Elisabeth idolized Anna. After progressing through many phases of her profession, working as a professional artist, fulfilling commissions, she won Anna Hyatt Huntington Prizes in 1970 and 1976. She founded the Lyme Academy and was instrumental in developing it into today's College of Fine Arts. She still teaches several courses in sculpture annually at Lyme Academy, College of Fine Arts, Old Lyme, Connecticut.

To Dr. David B. Dearinger who, when he was Chief Curator of the National Academy of Design at 1083 Fifth Avenue, New York, gave us a personal tour of the Academy, once Archer Huntington's home. He is now Susan Morse Hillem Curator of Paintings and Sculpture at the Boston Athenaeum.

To Robert W. Hoge, Curator of Coins, and Francis D. Campbell, Librarian, at the American Numismatic Society, who showed us Archer's collection of 30,355 ancient coins, including the rare Visigothic coins.

To Roberta Jeffries who found for us the W. W. Norton book published 1947 with photographs of Anna's sculptures and the names of museums which owned them. This helped with compiling a marketing list.

To Don Studley, CPA and history buff, who researched for us when the charitable gift tax deduction was enacted into law.

To Susan E. Smith, Research and Development Coordinator of the Palisades Interstate Parkway, who helped us with the Rocas story and provided photographs.

To Harlan Jessup, genealogist, who found the Hyatt genealogy, and located the news story dated November 16, 1928, in the *New York Times* about the visit of the Infante and Infanta of Spain to New York, an important event for the Huntingtons.

To Robin Salmon, Vice President and Curator of Sculpture at Brookgreen Gardens, South Carolina, for her patience and kind attention to our questions.

To Susan Harris, librarian at the Collis P. Huntington Memorial Library in Oneonta, New York, for informing us on the early Collis years.

To Thomas L. Cheney, lawyer, who handled the estates of both Anna and Archer. We thank him for his patient attention to our questions about the Huntingtons.

To Josh Graml, reference librarian at Mariners' Museum, who helped us through its maze of documents and photographs.

To Eileen Jelinski, assistant town clerk in Redding, who helped us with the Huntingtons' probate records.

To Andrea Zimmermann, librarian, writer, and knowledgeable editor and friend, who helped us shape our early ideas into a published book.

To Mary Maki who did the Index, an enthusiastic and competent friend.

To Marian and Wally Wood who kindly helped with marketing plans.

INTRODUCTION

Writing the story of Anna and Archer Huntington's marriage came about when we made the following discoveries. Whereas a great deal had been written about Anna and her career as a sculptor, little was available telling about Archer and his identity as a bibliophile, Hispanic scholar, poet, businessman, multimillionaire, philanthropist, and above all, a devoted and generous husband. They were married March 10, 1923, when Anna was 47 and Archer, 54. Archer died in 1955, and Anna, in 1973.

In 1990, we were assembling a book of hiking trails in Newtown and wanted to include the Collis P. Huntington State Park of 828 acres. Most of it is in Redding, Connecticut, but about thirty acres spilled over into Newtown, enough to justify including it in our book. The Huntington file at the Mark Twain Library in Redding told us that the park was named for Archer's father and that it had once been the estate where Anna and Archer had lived and died. This information was useful, but did not stir us to pursue the search.

Then in the millennium year a friend told us about visiting a spectacular park in South Carolina named Brookgreen Gardens founded by Archer and Anna Huntington. Some 500 pieces of sculpture including works not only by Anna, but also by many other contemporary American sculptors are set up in a natural lowland setting. Furthermore, the park is enormous, comprising about 9100 acres, represent-

ing four rundown colonial plantations built around 1700 and collectively called "Brookgreen." In 1930 the Huntingtons bought it and built a winter home near the ocean, a one-story U-shaped residence Archer named "Atalaya," an Arabic word meaning watch-tower.

As they developed the gardens using native labor, and placing Anna's sculptures here and there, they found that Brookgreen's lowland landscape and spreading live oaks formed an ideal outdoor setting for a garden and for sculpture. Falling in love with coastal South Carolina, they invited other sculptors to show their work there. The result is one of the most unusual and beautiful parks in the United States.

Surprised and now intrigued, we had to find out more about this unusual pair. In November 2000 we visited the Gardens. They were indeed stunning. But to our profound disappointment we found little about the Huntingtons published and for sale at the gift shop. Nor did the employee who helped us know more than what a simple informative brochure could reveal. We had a similar experience at the Mariners' Museum in Norfolk, Virginia, another of Archer Huntington's projects.

After sixty years as a journalist and finding answers to questions, Mary was frustrated. The Huntingtons were obviously accomplished, superior people. They must have left their marks in many places. Where did they come from? What did they do for the public good? Where had they lived and died? Why did they choose to live in the estate that was now Huntington State Park? Was it a happy marriage?

Yet no one had written their story. To find answers became compelling. Although we did not know then, in December 2000, what would be involved to satisfy our curiosity, we committed ourselves to research and writing a book about Anna and Archer Huntington.

Among the many sources we eventually consulted, the *Anna Hyatt Huntington Papers 1887–1973* in their entirety and some of the *Archer Milton Huntington Papers 1919–1957* stored in the Special Collections Archives at Syracuse University in Syracuse, New York, have been the most productive. Anna was a compulsive diarist. Her diaries start with January 1, 1925, two years after her marriage, and continue with only a few gaps through Archer's death, December 11, 1955. On Sunday, January 31, 1965, without explanation, she abruptly stopped, after forty years and forty-five days of noting daily temperatures and weather, outside events that concerned her and daily happenings in her life as well as in Archer's. We have read each diary, page-by-page, from 1925 through Archer's death, thirty all told.

The spine of our narrative is based entirely on Anna's account as to what happened. She never looked back or ahead. She simply documented the present with wit, humor, empathy, and an eye for telling detail. She rarely touted herself, except in one instance, when Archer had left his keys locked in his office. She broke the window to climb in and retrieve them. "Not bad for 66!" she wrote.

The *Papers* at Syracuse were also the source for many photographs of the Huntingtons, for letters to Anna, business correspondence, blueprints of their house named Stanerigg built in 1941, and articles about Anna's Scottish deerhound kennels.

Mary Mitchell wrote the text of this book. Albert Goodrich transcribed each diary to facilitate using it, and also worked out the diagram of Stanerigg Farm as Anna developed it during World War II time. He wrote the Postscript, collected and organized the photographs, created a database of Anna's sculptures, created maps, and provided logistical and technical support from start to finish. A final initiative was getting in touch with as many of Anna's extended family as we could find who were alive and willing to communicate with us. This was a fruitful and most enjoyable effort.

We became so devoted to Anna and Archer that we dedicated our book to their memory.

CHAPTER I

"THE HEROIC COUPLE"

1923–1925

IN THE EARLY 1920S a strange coincidence took place on a train to New York that would unite the lives of two remarkable people. Each day as Anna Hyatt, the famous sculptor, traveled to her studio in Greenwich Village, she noticed an elegant, unusually tall businessman boarding the train at the Eastchester station. He had a handsome, middle-aged face with a moustache and carried a voluminous briefcase. He would sit, take out papers and read all the way into New York. Although Anna was in her forties, she wasn't inclined towards marriage (her sister claimed her only love was sculpture). But for the first time in her life, she was observing a man without looking at him through "sculptor's eyes."[1]

"Who is he?" she would ask herself everyday on the train.

It would not be long before she found out, and it was the mutual love of art and fine craftsmanship that would unveil the mystery.

The fame of Anna Hyatt was already established. Her childhood on her family's farm at Annisquam, in northeast Massachusetts, had brought out a native love of animals, and mostly, of horses. She studied their bodies and how they moved in all poses on the farm, and then studied animals of every kind in the same way at the Boston Zoo. Drawn to sculpture as an artistic medium, even before she was twenty years old, Anna began crafting animals for sale with such ease and competence that around 1900 examples of her work appeared in the windows of the jewelry company of Shreve, Crump and Low in Boston. In 1902 she had her first one-artist show at the Boston Art Club.[2] It was the Gilded Age, and many wealthy patrons seeing her work, bought her animal pieces and even began to collect them. By 1912 she was distinguished as one of twelve American women earning $50,000 a year.[3]

Financially independent, she had gone to Paris where artists went to soak up its artistic atmosphere. Here she was naturally drawn to the concept of crafting a statue of Joan d'Arc on her militant warhorse. Anna always wanted her work to challenge her. She wrote, "I live in fear that I may some day be satisfied with what I do. Then I will know that I am no longer an artist."[4] Entering a model of Joan d'Arc in the Paris Salon of 1910 would be a risk, for in those days women did not tackle anything as formidable as an equestrian statue. She was also a foreigner. Finding the challenge irresistible, she started modeling the statue.

Jeanne d'Arc by Anna Vaughn Hyatt at Blois, France. Presented in 1922, it is a replica of the original *Jeanne d'Arc* which won Hon. Mention in the Paris Salon of 1910. Credit, Émile Schaub-Koch. *L'œuvres d'Anna Hyatt Huntington.* 1949. p. iii.

LEFT: *Portrait of Anna Vaughan Hyatt* 1915 by Marion Boyd Allen. Collection of Maier Museum of Art, Randolph-Macon Woman's College.

"For Anna, Joan's steed was all-important. She didn't want a draft animal. She wanted one active and heavy enough to bear the weight of Joan's armor. A long search ended when she saw the handsome stallions pulling delivery wagons from the stables of the Magasin du Louvre in Paris; one of these, a Percheron, became her model. Piece by piece, the statue was completed in four months, without assistance, in seven-day weeks of ten hours each day. She shut herself up in her studio, doing all the manual work herself, building her own armature, and amassing on it more than a ton of clay. She entered her model, a life-size plaster cast, in the Salon and won Honorable Mention."[5]

By this time Anna Hyatt's reputation in the American artistic community was well-known. In 1911, the Joan d'Arc Statue committee was formed to honor the Maid of Orleans on the 500th anniversary of her birth and to foster Franco-American friendship. Its Honorary President was J. Sanford Saltus, an executive of Tiffany and Company who had seen Anna's Joan d'Arc at the Paris Salon and been very much impressed.[6] So it was not surprising that she received the commission to create another equestrian Joan d'Arc for New York City. In 1915, while war raged in France, her statue was unveiled on December 6, 1915, at a site on Riverside Drive and 93rd Street.[7] An anomalous sight in that enclave of ordinary apartments and shops, it still stands there, alien and defiant in its medieval grandeur.

A few years later, a famous patron of the arts, Archer Milton Huntington, wanted to have a medal cast to honor the Centenary of the great Argentine patriot, Bartholomé Mitre, the founding editor of *La Nación*, a prominent liberal newspaper of the 1870s.

Mitre Medal honoring Bartholomé Mitre, 1921. Front (l), obverse (r). Courtesy, The Hispanic Society of America, New York.

Though he had never met Anna, Archer had followed her career as a sculptor. Wanting to promote women's place in the Arts, he commissioned Anna to design the medal for the Hispanic Society of America, of which he was founder and president. Anna and Archer agreed to meet at the Hispanic Society to discuss the project. It was sometime in 1921.[8]

That day Anna dressed more carefully than usual. She had heard a lot about Archer Milton Huntington, how, as a young man, this millionaire had traveled all over Spain for two years, become bilingual, fallen in love with the country and its people, and then returned home to establish the Hispanic Society in 1904. He had financed its large classic building out of his own pocket. She had never seen a photograph of him. So it was a surprise that morning to find at the Hispanic Society, standing up to greet her, the gentleman from the train—Archer Huntington, himself.

He asked if they had ever met.

Blushing, Anna replied, "Yes, on the train, coming to New York. We see each other every day."

"That's true!" said Archer. "I recognize you!"[9]

The next year, Anna and Archer met to consult about another Hispanic Society project—an outdoor exhibit of the National Sculpture Society to be held on the terrace in front of the Society. Anna was in charge of arrangements, and often had to consult with Archer. Their acquaintance deepened into friendship and, without being aware of it, they grew fond of each other. As Cuban journalist José García-Mazas put it, they found themselves "imprisoned in Cupid's embrace." And all much to the surprise of Archer's friends.[10]

You see, Archer was a divorced man. His friends thought he would never marry again. It was in 1895, in London, that he had married his first cousin, Helen Manchester Gates, daughter of Ellen, the youngest sister of Archer's father, Collis P. Huntington. A pretty, stylish young woman who loved jewels and furs, she was artistic and interested in theatre. As time passed, she grew bored with Archer's hobbies of traveling to Spain, collecting Visigothic coins and digging out Roman ruins near Italica, a town south of Seville. A worker there told García-Mazas how indifferent she had been to what her husband was doing. "She rarely came to see the excavations, and when she did, she would be 'all dressed up.'"[11] Traveling with Archer's mother, the wealthy Arabella Huntington, shopping and going to restaurants and the theatre, she didn't spend much time with her husband.

In New York, Helen's love for the theatre and society life separated her from Archer. He hated cocktail parties and black-tie affairs; she could not be happy without them. While Helen loved seeing her name in the society columns, Archer said, "If to become famous all I have to do was bend my index finger, I would not do it."[12] This explains why he threw out most newspaper columnists and radio station reporters from his house and never granted interviews.

Before the end of World War I Helen asked her husband for a divorce. Family tradition has it that she left a note on his dressing-table, saying she was leaving him to marry Granville Barker, a theatrical impresario. Archer's pride was devastated, his manly dignity violated. Bitterly, he recalled how at Helen's request he had entertained this very man at dinner in their home at 1083 Fifth Avenue. The blow shattered his poetic soul and made his dedication to his Hispanic endeavors seem trivial. Everything fell apart. He saw himself as having been made to appear as a cuckold. Growing sour and hostile, he closed himself off in his world of Hispanic culture, his only solace. The divorce took place in 1918. Believing his faith in women was permanently broken, his friends thought he would never marry again.

At length, he did crawl out of his shell to travel to Argentina in 1921 and presented the Mitre medal. On return he gradually reentered his familiar world of Hispanic Society enterprise and became acquainted with Anna, a sympathetic, competent woman of simple tastes, with a strong, single-minded focus on her art.

Much later, after Archer's death, at a memorial gathering at the Library of Congress, Washington, D.C., Brantz Mayor, Anna's nephew whom Archer had also been fond of, told a memorable story. He described how he discovered something was happening between Anna and Archer in the winter of 1922.

"One day I came into Aunt Anna's studio in Greenwich Village and found this enormous man with a large bunch of flowers wrapped in transparent paper in his hands. She was nearby working on some plasticene animal as they talked. She so often did that with close friends. Archer started to rise, but Aunt Anna told him to stay seated. I liked him instantly but felt I was interrupting something important, so left very soon.

"The next flashback," continued Brantz, "comes in the summer of 1922 at Annisquam where Anna grew up and where we gathered every summer. At breakfast she was missing. Ma said that Aunt Anna had left at dawn to catch the first train to Boston and then New York. During the night she had been awakened by such a strong premonition that Archer Huntington was dying that she simply had to go to New York and find out if this was true. This precipitous act was so out of character that I was stunned."[13]

Family history has it that she found him in a hospital, trying to regain his health. To forget the bitter past he had thrown himself into all manner of projects in his Hispanic world, in the midst of his collections, isolating himself from friends, and was exhausted.

Time can and does heal most wounds. The National Sculpture Society had asked him to organize an outdoor exhibit of American sculpture on the Audubon Terrace in front of the Hispanic Society, the American Numismatic Society and the American Academy of Arts and Letters. It was to open April 14, 1923, and run until August. On the committee was Anna Hyatt. Since they often had to consult together, they found themselves, as José García-Mazas wrote in his biography of Archer, "captivated by Cupid, without even being aware of it. Everyone had noticed that the Hispanist was once more himself, better than before."[14]

As for Anna, though in her mid-forties, she had found herself in love for the first time. When he first asked her to marry him, she had hesitated, not wanting to give up her simple, dedicated way of life. But sensing his acute need of her, and recognizing that she had already had a fulfilling career as an independent artist, she relented, and they were married on the 10th of March. They shared the same birthday. In this way, in the future, they could have three celebrations in one, calling every March 10 their "3-in-1 Day."

The marriage took place in the morning in her little studio at 49 West 12th Street in Greenwich Village. Only her mother, her sister, Harriet Hyatt Mayor, Harriet's two sons, A. Hyatt and Brantz Mayor, Brenda Putnam, a sculptor, and one or two others were there. The Reverend Pastor, Dr. Benjamin Bulkley, a Hyatt cousin, married them. Archer was so nervous that Harriet giggled when she heard Dr. Bulkley offer his shoulder as a prop for this huge man to lean on if necessary. The teasing helped Archer regain his composure. The news did not reach the newspapers until the couple was on a yacht waiting to take them to the Bahamas.[15] When they returned they became known as "The Heroic Couple," Archer as Titan because of his size and Anna as Diana because of the beauty of her recent sculpture, *Diana of the Chase*.[16]

1. José García-Mazas. *El Poeta y La Escultora*. Hispanic Society of America. 1962. 457.

2. David B. Dearinger. "Anna Hyatt Huntington." *American National Biography*, v. 11. 457.

3. Harold Hornstein. "In the Heroic and Classic Mold." *Yankee Magazine*. August 1970. 56.

4. Doris E. Cook. *Woman Sculptor: Anna Hyatt Huntington (1876–1973)*. 3. Prepared with the support of the Connecticut Commission on the Arts through the Connecticut Foundations for the Arts. Hartford: October 1973.

5. Ibid., 4.

6. Ibid., 4.

7. Ibid., 4.

8. G-M. *El Poeta*. 458.

9. Ibid., 462.

10. Ibid., 460.

11. Ibid., 460.

12. Ibid., 461.

13. Brantz Mayor. "Uncle Archer." Reminiscence read at the Library of Congress, Washington, D.C., at a memorial gathering after AMH's death. Manuscript in Huntington file, Mark Twain Library, Redding, Connecticut.

14. G-M. *El Poeta*. 462.

15. Ibid., 462.

16. *History of Collis P. Huntington Park*. Newtown Trails Book, 1991. C. H. Booth Library, Newtown, Connecticut. Text for Map 7.

CHAPTER 2

EL CID,
ARCHER'S FATHER,
AND ARABELLA'S PALACE

1926–1927

AFTER RETURNING from their honeymoon, Archer and Anna decided to embark on a major project. Anna would create an equestrian statue of El Cid Campeador, Spain's most famous military captain, and then she and Archer would present this gift to the nation at the International Exposition set for the spring 1929. Archer wanted to begin developing the Hispanic Society museum into a first-class institution. In 1904 after establishing it with a constitution and a board of directors, he bought land for its building. This was on West 155th Street in New York, on a commanding site overlooking the Hudson River called Audubon Terrace. The property had once been part of John James Audubon's farm, a sanctuary for the naturalist from 1839 until his death in 1851. With substantial assistance from his mother, Arabella Huntington, he funded a building on the site to house the Hispanic Society. The beautiful structure in the classic style was completed in 1908.

It embodied a childhood dream. "While staying with his mother in one of the great hotels in Rome, he walked miles each day through the huge museums there housing evidences of Italy's past greatness. He

could dream of nothing else but having a museum of his own. Cutting out of magazines pictures that touched his imagination, he mounted them on cardboard. Then he got the concierge to give him empty packing-boxes which he piled on their sides to form two lines of facing shelves. Then he arranged his cut-out treasures and made an imposing pair of gates by painting an iron-work design on scraps of cardboard. Above them he hung a sign reading 'Museum,' in uneven boyish letters, and invited his mother to see the show. The boy grew up and never lost his insatiable passion for museums."[1] He has been building them ever since, the Hispanic Society museum being the first of some fifteen or more in this country and elsewhere.

But the Hispanic Society was in America. Archer wanted to contribute something grand to be located in Spain, itself, to show his gratitude for giving him an enduring, rich focus for his life. After his marriage, and finding Anna wanted to share his interest, the Huntingtons decided the gift would be an equestrian statue of El Cid.

El Cid was actually a sobriquet by which Roderigo

Diaz Devivar (c.1043–1099) was known. An epic poem about El Cid had survived through the ages and been kept sequestered in a vault in Madrid. Archer got permission to withdraw it for study, and after ten years, produced such a remarkable translation from the old Castilian into English that Yale, Harvard, and Columbia universities each conferred on him an honorary degree for his achievement. Anna noticed how proud he was of this endeavor, and so suggested a statue of El Cid. For Anna a commission was like the clang of a bell to an old-time fire-horse. She started immediately to model the horse in clay.

While Anna became occupied with her model, Archer threw himself, heart and soul, into elevating the Hispanic Society and its museum into the first-class institution he envisioned. He had started its collections with his own library of thousands of books acquired in Spain years ago. While traveling through that mountainous country, Archer learned the culture of ancient Iberia and became bilingual not only in Spanish but also in the ancient Castilian language. He became interested in local customs and regional dress, and mediaeval art and books. His express purpose in founding the society was "advancement of the study of Spanish and Portuguese languages, literature, and history, and advancement of the study of the countries wherein Spanish and Portuguese are or have been spoken languages."[2]

Once his own collections were transported to and arranged in the new building, other collections snowballed. So many hundreds of photographs and prints, rare incunabula, woodcuts, embroideries and lace, ancient title-pages, etc. were acquired that a wing had to be added to the main building to house

Aerial View of Audubon Terrace, 1930. Credit, *The History of the Hispanic Society of America*, 1954.

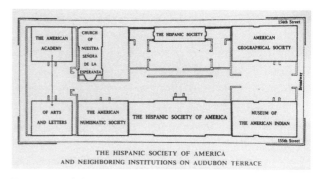

Layout Audubon Terrace. Credit, *The History of the Hispanic Society of America*, 1954.

and display them. This meant hiring a staff to catalog everything.

Despite a widespread feeling to the contrary, Archer wanted to show that women could be scholarly and could administer an institution. His attitude contrasted with that of his cousin, Henry E. Hun-

22

El Cid Group by Anna Hyatt Huntington, 1927, in HSA courtyard. Print from *The History of the Hispanic Society of America*, 1954.

tington, who funded the renowned Huntington Library, Art Collections, and Botanical Gardens in San Marino, California. Henry, like Collis before him, scorned women as librarians and administrators. Archer was just the opposite. He felt women could master detail better than men and could administer effectively. His main requirement was that whatever they did must not be sloppy. It must be scholarly. "Staff shall also know words and sayings and have met native creatures near to men, from mule to bedbug."[3] He also hired the handicapped and underprivileged. For instance, one curator, Florence May Lewis, a graduate of Gallaudet College for the Deaf in Washington, D.C., became a noted specialist in lace, embroidery, and fabrics. "For as

long as anyone remembers," writes Dr. Gerald J. MacDonald, Librarian at the Society, "he strove to hire black and Hispanic personnel from the immediate neighborhood around W. 155th Street."[4]

In the midst of Archer's administrative work and Anna's sculpting, something unexpected forced them to shove all plans to the back burners. In the spring of 1924, Archer's mother Arabella became ill, and he dropped everything to take care of her. After all, it was Arabella who had brought him up to be a cultivated scholar and speak fluent French and Spanish. She had married his father Collis and financed his travels in northern Spain. And it was due to her generosity that six buildings and a church were built on Audubon Terrace to house his collections and promote his special interests. Four of the buildings were the Hispanic Society of America, the American Numismatic Society, the American Geographic Society, and the Museum of the American Indian. A Spanish church dedicated to Nuestra Señora de la Esperanza fronted on W. 156th Street, the northern boundary of the Terrace. Other buildings Arabella financed were for the National Institute of Arts and Letters, and for the American Academy of Arts and Letters, an offspring of the Institute. The aim of these two groups, which Archer himself wholeheartedly believed in, was "to further the interest of literature and the fine arts." He was elected to each, to the Institute in 1911 and the Academy in 1922. As a writer for *The New Yorker* put it some fifty years later, Audubon Terrace had become "a kind of Parnassus,"[5] and Archer and Arabella were proud of it.

In September, Arabella died, and Archer as co-executor of her will began to handle probate proceedings. (Henry E. Huntington, Arabella's second

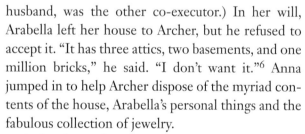

Don Quixote, bas-relief on courtyard wall mounted 1942, print from *The History of the Hispanic Society of America*, 1954.

Boabdil bas-relief on courtyard wall mounted 1943, print from *The History of the Hispanic Society of America*, 1954.

husband, was the other co-executor.) In her will, Arabella left her house to Archer, but he refused to accept it. "It has three attics, two basements, and one million bricks," he said. "I don't want it."[6] Anna jumped in to help Archer dispose of the myriad contents of the house, Arabella's personal things and the fabulous collection of jewelry.

Archer knew that No. 2 East Fifty-seventh Street was already a white elephant. In 1895 when Arabella and Collis chose the site to build a new home, the area was the most fashionable residential district in New York. But in the wake of World War I the section of Fifth Avenue from 50th north to 59th Street, was rapidly acquiring a commercial veneer. The wrecker's ball had demolished three of the several Vanderbilt palaces and other homes of the Four Hundred (the leaders of New York society) dotting the Avenue. With chic new specialty shops and office buildings replacing the mansions built by the carriage trade in the 1880s, the stretch of the Avenue called the Upper Fifties was becoming the "parade-ground of the middle class." Window-shopping at the eye-catching displays in the new or renovated shops had become an escape from the drudgery of home life.[7]

Another kind of escape for the middle class was available on the long cross-streets between Fifth and

Sixth avenues. In 1925, along West Fifty-second Street, F. Scott Fitzgerald's bootlegger friend Gatsby would have felt right at home as the Prohibition Era was in full swing. "It amused many New Yorkers that the city's most notable concentration of speakeasies was not far from the ugly brownstone palace at 640 Fifth Avenue built by the heir of Commodore Vanderbilt in 1879 and 1880, and now occupied by the Commodore's grandson and his wife, Mr. and Mrs. Cornelius Vanderbuilt III. West Fifty-second Street between Fifth and Sixth Avenues, was notorious throughout the country. Almost without exception, every house, on both sides of the street between Fifth and Sixth, was a speak, and the after-dark traffic on this single block was always more congested than that on any so-called 'residential' cross street in Manhattan."[8]

(Guests of Cornelius Vanderbilt III and his hospitable, lively wife, Grace, must have been thankful that they could enter the palace from Fifth Avenue through the glass vestibule entrance.)

Acutely aware of the changes that had taken place, Archer was anxious to cut his ties to the once-familiar neighborhood and belong to it only in memory.

By this time you may wonder about Archer's heritage, the source of his fortune and who his father was, for he was born out of wedlock. There are two versions of that story. The first was Archer's who told it to A. Hyatt Mayor, Anna's nephew, whom he liked and trusted. Hyatt was Curator of Prints at the Metropolitan Museum of Art.

Collis was the dominant partner in California's legendary Big Four. During the six years 1863–1869 they were building the railroads, Collis was the workhorse, traveling between New York and Wash-

Print of Collis Potter Huntington from the photographs in *El Poeta y La Escultora* by José García-Mazas. Published by the Hispanic Society of America, 1962.

ington, D.C., to arrange for financing for the enterprise and to work with the federal government. The Big Four had President Abraham Lincoln's support. This quadrumvirate pushed through the Central Pacific Railroad from Sacramento, California, to meet the Union Pacific, which had started west from Omaha, Nebraska. The tracks met at Promontory,

Oswald Birley painted both portraits in the same year, 1924. In her will Arabella left her portrait to her son Archer. The Hispanic Society of America owns it now. The Huntington Library and Art Collections in San Marino, California, owns the portrait of its founder, Henry Edwards Huntington. Arabella's first husband was Collis P. Huntington. Her second, whom she married in 1913, was Collis's nephew, Henry E. Huntington.

Utah, and on May 10, 1869, the historic Golden Spike was driven into the ground. Collis became very wealthy from this endeavor and afterward, devoted himself to creating a network of railroads crisscrossing the nation from south to north.

Developing the Chesapeake & Ohio Railroad, based in Richmond, was part of his work. When in Richmond he stayed at a boardinghouse run by Richard Milton Yarrington and his wife, Catherine J. Yarrington. They had a bright and attractive daughter

named Arabella Duval Yarrington who was about nineteen or twenty years old. With his wife Elizabeth an invalid in their house at 65 Fifth Avenue in New York City, Collis persuaded Arabella to join his household and take care of her.

They fell in love, and she bore him a son on March 10, 1870. To name him Arabella took the middle name of two people close to her, John Archer Worsham, a proprietor of a gambling house in Richmond, and her father to arrive at Archer Milton

26

Worsham. Arabella called herself Mrs. Belle D. Worsham, the name she stuck to until she married Collis on July 12, 1884. (Elizabeth died of cancer in October 1883.)[9] Soon Archer asked if he could take the Huntington name. Collis enthusiastically agreed, calling him "my son" ever afterward but never formally adopting him.[10]

The second version was Arabella's. Various other authoritative sources tell about it. She said she had married Mr. Worsham and when she became pregnant, followed him to New York where he planned to start up a new gambling parlor. The Yarrington family followed her and established another boardinghouse where Arabella gave birth to her son. The 1870 census taken in June listed the occupants of the Yarrington boardinghouse. One is Bell De Worsion, another John De Wershion, and an infant named John De Version. Thirty-two days later, in July, Worsham is listed in the Richmond census as John A. Worsham, head of a household that included his wife, Annette. Signatures dated on land record deeds and tax rolls in Richmond revealed he had been married to Annette since at least 1866. She died in 1874 and he in 1878. Arabella never knew about Annette. (All his life Archer was certain that his name was Archer, not John, and that he had been born in New York City, not in Virginia, as the census entry states.)[11]

If you are confused, you are not alone. Cerinda W. Evans (1876–1973), the highly respected, longtime librarian at the Mariners' Museum in Newport News, Virginia, retired in 1948 and then wrote a two-volume biography of Collis Potter Huntington, which Archer was very pleased with. While doing this, Miss Evans ran into the contradictions and half-

2 East Fifty-seventh Street, New York City. Built in 1895 by Collis P. Huntington and his second wife, Arabella. Demolished 1926.

truths of Arabella's story. Blessed with the true librarian's tenacity in research and probably admiring the young mother's courage, she dug around in municipal archives, city directories, census, and judicial records, trying to ferret out the truth. Eventually, she wrote a brief account of her search. After Archer's death, the Museum made it available in 1956. The manuscript does not circulate.

Despite her tireless efforts Miss Evans found no birth certificate for Arabella, none for Archer, no licence for Arabella's marriage to Worsham. After Arabella died in 1924, there was no obituary. No matter who writes Arabella's story, either following Miss Evans's path or digging elsewhere, hoping to turn up a new clue, he or she bumps up against the same lack of documentation. So considering these legal barriers, Archer's paternity will undoubtedly never be certified.

Certainly his height and intellectual powers

matched those of the tall, robust and dynamic Collis. So Archer's version, that the railroad magnate is Archer's father, is now generally accepted. If Anna knew the true story she never told it, for she was The Clam, a nickname her school friends gave her because she could be totally trusted.[12] But it wouldn't have mattered to Anna, for all her life she liked people for what they were and not for their background or family tree. Archer, on the other hand, frankly admitted he was illegitimate and has been alleged to have said to a friend, "I am a bastard."[13]

Arabella's second husband, Henry E. Huntington, was Collis's nephew. He had a lavish estate and house in San Marino, California. When he and Arabella married in 1913, they split their time between San Marino, where he preferred to be, and Arabella's home in New York at 2 East Fifty-seventh Street. After Collis's death in 1900, and even after marrying Henry Huntington, Arabella's huge greystone building, which architectural critics enjoyed calling a railroad depot, remained her primary residence. She loved the place. There she could see Archer, who, as her only offspring, was ever her adored child. Once when a friend was visiting, he saw Arabella stick her head out of her bedroom doorway and call, "Where's my baby?" "Here I am, Mother," came the answer as a heavily bearded man (namely, Archer) bounded up the stairs to see her.[14]

Arabella had given Archer $1000 a month while he was in his teens ($19,000 in 2003 money).[15] Then in his early twenties, she increased his allowance to finance his Spanish travels and set up five trusts for him in 1897 at the Union Trust Company of New York. Two years later she deeded him five more trusts valued at half a million each.[16]

In spite of her wealth and comfortable living, Arabella was not a happy woman. Ever since the 1890s, she had had severe headaches and depression due to her glaucoma. Today, remedies for this unfortunate disease are common, but then there were none. She compensated for this misfortune by buying all manner of valuable and rare paintings, tapestries, and jewels. After Collis died, Arabella wore only black, and bought or was given pearls and diamonds and other precious jewelry to brighten up her wardrobe and spirits.

Arabella became a frequent client of Sir Joseph Duveen, a knowledgeable broker of fine arts, who taught her quite a lot about his field. Through her heavy, thick glasses, she could see enough to apply this knowledge; after a time, she became a discriminating and respected collector. It's no wonder that on the Huntington walls hung the Beauvais tapestries and paintings by the old masters, Velázquez, Vermeer, and Goya.

On September 16, 1924, Arabella died at the age of 74. It took years to settle the estate. Details of the accounting were published in the *New York Times*, April 16, 1927. On the death of Collis P. Huntington, her first husband, Arabella had received $22 million plus the real estate described earlier; at the date of the accounting, the estate had increased by $2.8 million. After all expenses, the two co-executors were left with $18,749,822 to be divided equally.[17] Archer put his share into the stock market; we shall find out later what happened to that tidy sum.

The overwhelming number and character of its contents made clearing out 2 East Fifty-second Street an enormous task. Since it was first occupied in 1895 and until Arabella's death, almost thirty years later, three unusually acquisitive and rich people had lived there. First Collis and Arabella; then Arabella alone until 1913 when she married Henry Edwards Huntington, Archer's first cousin. Henry was such an avid collector of rare books, manuscripts, first editions et al. that in 1917 the *Boston Transcript* said he was "the first bibliophile in the land."[18] When he married Arabella in 1913 and moved into her house, the entire third floor was remodeled to accommodate his library of 40,000 volumes. Six male librarians who catalogued and arranged his books, and handled mail worked there every day.[19] Fortunately, the situation was temporary. In 1920 Henry shipped the books to San Marino, California, to the new library he had had built to house them.

This was like taking a bushel of hay out of a haystack. The mass left in Arabella's "railroad depot" was scarcely diminished. Years afterward, Anna wrote a description of how she and Archer had handled their part of the operation.

"When my much beloved Mother-in-law died in 1924," wrote Anna, "she left a very large collection of jewelry. Pearls, diamonds, emeralds, rubies, etc. After her death my husband said the box is yours if you want it. It was a box about 18 inches square, covered with leather and at least 8 trays of jewels. I looked at its contents with amazement, and I am afraid some repulsion as well. Having none of the normal feminine desires to dangle ornaments on my person or see capital tied up in these bits of glass with their false values and no value for education, sustenance, or income in them.

"Much to my husband's surprise, I said thanks very much, but if you don't mind I would rather not have them. He could not imagine a woman who would not want them. They had of course to be valued by experts to come into the Federal and State inheritance taxes and I well remember these jewelry experts sitting around a large table expertizing and listing those useless baubles as if they were something real. A year or so later these jewels were sold, and the buyers had gathered them into a heap looking for all the world like a glittering, many-colored fabulous scene from the Arabian Nights. I shall never forget the relief when this heap was no longer ours.

"There was not only the jewelry on our hands but her enormous collection of pictures, furniture, ceramics, silver, rugs, etc., the huge house at 2 East Fifty-seventh Street of 60 or more rooms with several of them storerooms piled high. But also the Westchester house of 50 furnished rooms, the Adirondacks Camp on Raquette Lake in upper NY State, a stable on Fifty-seventh Street; all these had to be sorted as to the most valuable to be given to museums and the rest sold at auction.

"It took several years before they were distributed to the right places. The Metropolitan got many pictures, some sculpture and furniture. The Yale Museum a large collection of furniture, the Palace of the Legion of Honor at San Francisco a large varied collection in memory of C.P.H.; the Huntington Museum in Pasadena, the collection of early Italian paintings. The sorting and moving I had to see to in a large part as my husband had his hands full with the details of settling the estate, selling of property and establishing of all these collections to museums as gifts, not counting his own numerous administrative duties of his institutions. These were terribly busy years, as I was also in the studio as much as possible doing the El Cid statue group for the Hispanic Society, with four large warrior figures to crouch at the four corners to give weight to the composition, the bases of two flag poles, the Red Doe and Fawn, life size, the Red Stag, life size, and about 30 smaller pieces."[20]

1. Edward Laroque Tinker, The Hispanic Society of America. 1958. 2. Reprinted by permission from THINK Magazine ©1953 by International Business Machines Corporation. Series IV, Box 1. *Published Material 1958–1960*. AHH Papers.

2. Beatrice Gilman Proske. *Archer Milton Huntington*. Hispanic Society of America. 1963. 8.

3. Ibid., 17.

4. Gerald J. MacDonald to Mary Mitchell (MM). 30 November 2001.

5. Geoffrey T. Hellman. "Some Splendid and Admirable People," Profile. *The New Yorker*. 23 February 1973. 44.

6. Thomas Cheney to MM. 4 September 2001.

7. Robert A. M. Stern. *New York 1930*. Rizzoli International Publications, Inc. 1987. 293, 308, 589.

8. Lloyd Morris. *Incredible New York: High Life and Low Life of the Last Hundred Years*. Random House. 1951. 326.

9. James Thorpe. *Henry Edwards Huntington: A Biography*. Berkeley. University of California, 1994. 308.

10. David Lavender. *The Great Persuader*. Niwot, Colorado. The University Press of Colorado. 1998. 346.

11. James T. Maher. *Twilight of Splendor*. Little, Brown & Co. Boston Toronto. 1975. 246–263. Chapter IV is entitled "San Marino." It gives a full account of the research into Ara-

bella Duval Worsham's life before she married Collis P. Huntington. The chapter also describes two residences: 1) Collis P. Huntington at 2 East Fifty-seventh Street, New York built 1892 and demolished 1926; and 2) the "ranch" built and occupied by Henry Edwards Huntington in San Marino, California, expanded and now known as The Huntington Library, Art Collections and Botanical Gardens.

12. A. Hyatt Mayor. *Introduction: A Century of American Sculpture*. Abbeville Press, Publishers. New York, 1988. 24.

13. Conversations with Gerald J. MacDonald, Mary Mitchell and Albert Goodrich. 7 September 2001.

14. James Thorpe. *Henry Edwards Huntington. A Biography*. University of California Press. Berkeley. 1994. 324.

15. "Chart 1." *Research Reports*. January 14, 2002. American Institute for Economic Research. Great Barrington, Massachusetts. 1.

16. Thorpe. 314, 323.

17. Cook. 16.

18. Thorpe. 351, 340–352.

19. Donald C. Dickinson. *Henry Huntington's Library of Libraries*. Huntington Library Press, 1995. 84.

20. Undated manuscript. Series I, Box I, Folder: "Biographical Material." AHH Papers.

CHAPTER 3

TOO MANY IRONS IN THE FIRE
1926–1928

ALTHOUGH ARCHER devoted a great deal of time to settling his mother's estate, he had other business to attend to. He wanted to begin clearing out the townhouse at 1083 Fifth Avenue that he and his first wife had bought in 1902 to be their primary residence. After Anna and Archer were married, they lived at 1083, but eventually, Archer wanted to offer the place to the National Academy of Design for office, storage, and display space. "The original building was one of two rowhouses constructed in 1901–02 as numbers 1082 and 1083 along the avenue, midblock between 89th and 90th streets and across from Central Park. Just as the buildings were being completed, Archer bought them, and had them redesigned in the elegant tradition of New York townhouses at the turn of the century."[1]

But twenty-five years had passed. Now, since marrying Anna, his point-of-view about property, its use, and his needs had changed. After his mother's death the year before, he had to dispose of her myriad possessions at 2 East Fifty-seventh Street and also, the real estate Arabella had inherited from Collis, her first husband. This was substantial. There was "The Homestead," a sprawling country home at Westchester outside New York City where she and Collis had lived during the late 1880s. In addition, there were the furnishings from the French chateau outside Paris, which Arabella had leased and refurbished, with her second husband, Henry Edwards Huntington, that were beginning to stack up at East Fifty-seventh Street. Anna's distaste for having to handle all these possessions became so strong she could not keep silent. "We want to simplify," she said. (D1925, December 31) Burdened as he was, Archer agreed with her.

So it was a Godsend that in March 1926 there should come on the market No. 1 East Eighty-ninth Street, a townhouse around the corner from 1083 Fifth Avenue. Here an office suite could be arranged for him. It was an ideal solution, and Archer bought it immediately. They could keep the larger rooms at 1083 for entertaining, and retain their personal rooms there until changes were made in No. 1 to suit their individual tastes. (D1926, April 2) Within a week of signing the deed, painters worked in the downstairs rooms. Carpenters converted another room into an office and moved two large safes into it. More carpenters equipped rooms upstairs with shelves and cases for Archer's books. (D1926, April 19, 27, 29; May 7, 13)

Anna was delighted for another reason. Ever since

1083 Fifth Avenue, New York City, The home of Archer M. Huntington from 1902–1940. In 1940 he deeded it to the National Academy of Design. Next to 1083 is The Church of Heavenly Rest, where the funeral of Archer Huntington was held. Photograph by A. S. Goodrich.

Northeast corner of East Eighty-ninth and Fifth Avenue, New York. The little canopy covers the entrance to No. 1 East Eighty-ninth Street, the Huntingtons' city perch after 1940. Credit, Anna Hyatt Huntington Papers, Syracuse University Library, Special Collections Center.

she and Archer had decided to give *El Cid* to Spain she had been working on the statue at a studio west of Central Park. (Its location is unclear.) During the "horrid" winter months when she wanted to work there she had to make the round-trip on foot through mud and ice. (D1925, February 11, 12) Furthermore, she couldn't get models to come and pose in an unheated cold studio. Having her studio at East Eighty-ninth, right where she lived, offered a much

more convenient arrangement. So plans for a studio in the "new" house on the fifth floor, and for a greenhouse on the sixth floor above were also made. The block and tackle later installed to raise heavy materials from the studio and lower it to a truck outside, can still be seen in the house.[2]

Spring was busy. Crates of books and business papers were brought over from 1083, and Archer spent a happy week arranging them on the new shelves of his library. Anna was bringing her personal things over to her room at No. 1 East Eighty-ninth. She had luncheon parties, and her mother came to visit. While she did not enjoy having tax-appraisers inspect Arabella's jewelry and the twenty-nine pieces of furniture earmarked for Yale University and the Metropolitan Museum, she was glad for the chance to select linens to send to Archer's cousins on the west coast. With his perverse sense of humor, Archer was relishing visits from a Spanish cardinal and seven prelates, all eager to meet him despite his status as a divorced man. He was publishing another book of poetry, and took great pleasure from checking galleys of the poems and remembering the Spanish images surging through his mind as he read the poems. Both Anna and Archer enjoyed a visit from Sir Joseph Duveen, the international art dealer, who was interested in two Murillos in Arabella's collection.

In fact, it could have been a pleasant, relaxing spring had it not been for a self-imposed, disruptive endeavor that had to be considered every time they wanted to plan anything. This was the fussy, bustling, persistent presence of José López Mezquita, the artist, whom Archer had commissioned to paint his and Anna's portraits. In February Anna and Archer went to an exhibition of his work as a portrait painter. (José María López Mezquita, 1883–1954, was born in Granada.) They must have been pleased with it and given him a commission, for on March 3 Mezquita arrived at 1083 with easel and paints to start Archer's portrait. In the portrait Archer wears a dark-colored formal business suit, the kind of suit he wore often and was comfortable in. He poses on the black and white parquet floor of the large salon at 1083, in a corner near a window that overlooks Eighty-ninth Street (now called the Stone Room), and today, the Guggenheim Museum, holding a thin little book bound in red against his hip.[3] Everything

went well, for Mezquita finished on April 9. The painting hangs today on the wall of Archer's office at the Hispanic Society, an imposing image of a huge, handsome, and proud man at ease with himself.

Painting Anna, however, was a different story. The first pose was on April 19. In the portrait she stands looking down at him, an aristocratic, statuesque woman, in a creamy-white satin, body-clinging gown, the image of the fashionable society matron, the woman Archer would like her to have been, but one she would never be or want to be. (Anna was always happiest in a comfortable old cotton or wool dress and sweater, or her smock hanging loosely around her hips.) Doubtless, Archer, not Anna, chose what she should wear. After twelve posings, "poor Mezquita was painting and repainting" the white satin gown (while Anna posed and posed). At length, either he, or perhaps Anna, suggested they put the satin gown on a mannequin, and let him paint what he then saw. (D1926, May 18) This solution worked. The painting went smoothly, and on June 26 Anna posed for the last time. For Anna spring may have brought some pleasure. But in essence, it was "nothing but hard work." (D1926, June 16)

The last straw came when relatives from the west coast en route to Europe wanted to stop and visit. Archer announced they were going to Camp Arbutus in the Adirondacks and would not be home. "The whole world is passing through," said Anna. "June is the worst month of the year." (D1926, June 16)

Throughout this busy time, Anna had deep anxieties about her health which she kept to herself. For several years she had had chronic colds and lingering bronchial infections. Nevertheless, being the dedicated artist that she was, she always put aside her

El Cid Campeador was placed in the Hispanic Society courtyard, August 15, 1927. It is a replica of the original *El Cid*, which was sent in 1927 to Seville, Spain.

worries in order to squeeze in every free moment in her studio.

The two statues of *El Cid* absorbed her attention. The first was a bronze-casting to be shipped to Spain in time for the Hispanic-American Exposition set to open in Seville in May 1929. King Alfonzo XIII had already invited Anna and Archer to Seville to see *El Cid* in place, and then visit Madrid to celebrate the gift. The Marqués de Vega Inclán, a friend of Archer's, would handle all arrangements.

The second *El Cid* was the focus of an ensemble that Archer wanted for the sunken courtyard at Audubon Terrace opposite the Hispanic Society's entrance. The medieval folk hero on his war horse was to command the center. Bronze statues of four nude male warriors would mark the corners. A tall flagpole with a carved base showing warriors, horses, and spears in frenzied confusion was to mark the scene. Flanking *El Cid*, mounted on the wall to its back, were to be two legendary Spanish figures carved in relief. To the left, Boabdil, the last King of the Moors, on his spirited Arab charger; to the right, Don Quixote, Cervantes' beloved visionary on Rocinante, his faithful steed, as they set out on their mission. A seated red stag with a crown of antlers was to mark the east flight of steps into the courtyard; a red doe and her fawn, the west flight. Anna wanted the group to be in place by the middle of 1927.

After spending the summer at Camp Arbutus in the Adirondacks, on return Anna found her studio at No. 1 ready for her to commence work. (D1926, October 17) During her absence El Cid, now full-size, had been tranferred from the former studio west of Central Park, to the new studio. Encouraged, Anna started to mold the first warrior.

But within a year she had to put away her tools. Working intensely on everything, she finally realized the congestion in her lungs was not going to improve and knew she had better visit her doctor for X-rays. On November 17, 1927, she wrote in her diary, "Lungs are affected. I have to stop and go away."

On hearing the diagnosis Anna had not acted surprised. She had grown up in a time when people with symptoms like hers, namely, chronic cough, cracklings in the lungs, low temperature, blood in the mucous discharge, were diagnosed as consumptives. "Phthisis, as the Greeks called consumption, is one of the oldest and most persistent diseases known to civilized man. From 1800 to 1870 tuberculosis was responsible for one in every five deaths in the United States. By the 1830s most Americans were familiar with it. The next generation (which was Anna's) knew how people dreaded it, how unpredictable and fatal it could be, and how many people and often a family, had pulled up stakes and trekked west to settle in the pure uncontaminated air of Colorado Springs or southern California. The West was settled just as much by consumptives seeking health in the great outdoors as by adventurers seeking their fortunes in gold or silver.

"In 1882 Robert Koch, a German bacteriologist, discovered the tubercle bacillus. Consumption gave way to tuberculosis, and the presence of bacilli in the sputum, as revealed on the laboratory slide, identified the disease. Decades were to pass, however, before doctors knew for certain what kind of treatment could bring about a lasting cure."[4] By the time Anna discovered she had the disease, therapy at a sanatorium like that at Saranac Lake in the Adirondacks had gained a reliable reputation.

The situation put her on the horns of an acute personal dilemma. She had been married to Archer only four years. They had embarked together on two enterprises that meant a great deal to him, and she was the only person who could bring them about.

In addition, they were planning a trip through Algeria and Morocco to Seville for the spring of 1929. The site for *El Cid* in the Andalusian capital had already been selected, a plaza named Glorieta San Diego where four major streets intersected. It would stand opposite the entrance gate to the Exposition park.[5]

She had two options. One was to stay home, cut down on activity, and try to get well. Or she could take a cure at a sanatorium that might last a year or so, but she would probably end up a healthy woman. Weighing these factors, one against the other, she and Archer decided to try the sanatorium in Asheville, North Carolina, famous since the 1880s as a health resort town with an altitude of 2310 feet above sea level. They would lease a house in Asheville, and staff it with the household people from No. 1 East Eighty-ninth Street. After making this decision, Archer completed writing his will and deposited it in the Central Trust Bank. Technicians came to wire his library and Anna's storeroom for security. Then they packed the car and departed, with return date unknown. (D1927, December 1)

The sanatorium was set in Biltmore Forest, the huge estate of George W. Vanderbilt (1862–1914), grandson of the "Commodore" and fourth son of the Commodore's heir, William H. Vanderbilt. Nearby they leased a large house and installed themselves and the staff, which consisted of Annie, their long-time housekeeper, three servants, and their pet white poodle named Winkler. Except for freight trains rumbling through the estate every night, quiet reigned. Remote from family, friends, and responsibilities, they came to love it. Archer could work on his correspondence amounting to some 100 letters daily without interruptions. Anna could concentrate on rest and recovery.

From the outset, though, much as they liked the setting, the doctor treating Anna rubbed her the wrong way. "His office in an old house is not sanitary; the waiting-room has spitmarks on the floor; the office looks like a college coed's room; fly specks pepper the old soiled furniture. He quite lost his temper with me and said that if I was not suited to my surroundings I was nothing but a spoiled, pampered rich woman. I mildly replied that I had earned my own living for twenty-five years. He said nothing after that for a while . . . Then he asked me to put down all thoughts, anything that troubled me, the more intimate the better. I must look into your eyes and teach you to develop will-power to resist pleasure and indulgences. I cannot give any opinion until I know your soul. In other words, no secrets from the dear Dr.—old fool. Archer sees that I am never alone with him." (D1928, January 6)

Anna may have found him abrasive and his consulting rooms offensive. But before two months had passed, she was recording improvement. From at first walking only fifteen minutes at a time, she succeeded in reaching twenty-five minutes without fatigue. The regular life proved to be good for Archer too. He had no indigestion, and he had given up smoking. Even Winkler was more energetic. When the weather cooperated they took drives through the network of mountainous roads, enjoying the views of the Great Smokies and observing signs of the scientific forestry methods Mr. Vanderbilt had initiated in the 1890s. Archer found some French books to read aloud in the evening. She read wild detective stories, and their Swedish cook cooked vegetables to perfection, helping Anna keep her weight down to 142 pounds.

By the end of March both Anna and Archer were fed up with the sanatorium routine and the atmosphere. In addition, Archer was anxious to return to projects he had initiated before leaving New York. With Anna's temperature normal for a week and the doctor's good news that her lung infection was now inactive, she was discharged. The Huntingtons packed up and departed. Their stay, despite its disagreeable aspects, had demonstrated how important altitude, rest, and breathing clean, fresh air were for recovery. "I may be better," said Anna as they left. "But nothing on earth would induce me to return." (D1928, April 3)

* * *

BACK HOME at No. 1 East Eighty-ninth Street, they faced the realities of living in New York. Anna had to finish carving the flagpole base for the *El Cid* ensemble. Carrie Campbell, Arabella's paid companion since 1887 and considered part of the family, was coming for a visit. This meant Carrie would have the car at her disposal and lunch with them four or five days in a row. In spite of interruptions, still convalescing, Anna kept up a routine. During their absence a sun-room had been built on the roof, and she initiated a routine of regular afternoon rest in the sun up there in the fresh air. A succession of sore throats, chest-colds and headaches plagued Archer. He refused to stay in bed, and Anna, aware that tuberculosis was contagious, hovered over him with a thermometer and frequent pleas to stay in bed. When he refused, she called their doctor to order him to do so. Archer remained a single day, and then, was off and running again.

Once on his feet, he faced the dentist, money-seekers, and organizations needing his guidance and inevitably, his financial support. Working with the Hispanic Society was always a pleasure. But the American Geographical Society's needs were giving

36

him a headache. This wasn't because he didn't believe in its mission. Fascinated by maps and voyages of discovery ever since adolescence he had been president of the organization from 1907 to 1911. At that time he and his mother financed buying a plot on Audubon Terrace and erecting on it an adequate headquarters for the Society. Now, in May at his bidding, its current president, Dr. Isaiah Bowman and fourteen members of the board met at No. 1. Hearing that the Society was in the red, Archer gave it $200,000. In the future, he said, it would have to stand on its own feet. No more money. "I do not think it right," he said, "that the institution should be known to depend on one man. It's a bad policy." (D1928, May 7)

The next important visitor was Sir Joseph Duveen, the international art dealer who had helped Arabella Huntington build up her distinguished art collection. He wanted to bargain with Archer to buy back its most outstanding painting. This was Rembrandt's *Aristotle Contemplating the Bust of Homer* painted in 1653 for a Sicilian nobleman, Don Antonio Ruffo.[6] In 1907 it had turned up in Paris in the Rudolph Kann Collection, which Duveen bought in its entirety. According to history, in the Duveen firm's archives in London, an Hungarian Count Baltazzi had been given ten thousand pounds to interest Arabella in looking at the collection. He succeeded. Heading the list of paintings was the *Aristotle*. Arabella bought it, and at her death, Archer inherited it. He loaned it to the Metropolitan Museum of Art to hang with two portraits by Franz Hals, which were also legacies from his mother. The *Aristotle* soon became the most famous painting to hang on the museum's walls.[7]

Now Duveen wanted to buy it back. After two visits and "much throwing up of hands and various dramatics," he agreed to pay $680,000, the price Archer quoted him for the three paintings. The next day Archer received a check for $660,000 along with Duveen's demand that the three pictures be delivered to him right away. "Archer had told the Metropolitan people not to let Duveen have them," wrote Anna. "But his man came this a.m. and said Archer had authorized him to take the pictures away. They were weak-kneed enough to let them go." (D1928, May 15–19) Despite the discrepancy Archer accepted Duveen's check for $660,000 and deposited it.

Anna, who was present during these meetings, observed the entire transaction in silence. But in her diary she expressed her dismay at how this eminent dealer of Dutch-Jewish extraction had taken advantage of Archer. "We made the mistake of not having him write his promise to pay 680 before he left the house. Dealing with a Jew is an eye-opener," she wrote. The final chapter in this episode took place when Duveen sent the Huntingtons a Goya *Portrait of a Woman* for them to try in their library. "It's well," wrote Anna, "to have a picture of his in the house if he tries tricks on us again." (D1928, May 19)

Being the canny collector that he was, Archer undoubtedly knew he was being fleeced. But it didn't bother him because he now had the cash on hand to move forward with a project he had had in mind for some time. This was constructing a building on the north side of Audubon Terrace for the American Academy of Arts and Letters.

To understand Archer's tie with this select institution, we have to backtrack. In 1911 he was elected to the National Institute of Art and Letters, its prede-cessor, and an organization of 250 members. But before long, its large size came to mean that not enough dignity could be bestowed on individual members. So it was decided there should be a smaller and more exalted body, this time on the model of the French Academy. The American Academy got underway in 1904. From the Institute's rolls, fifty were selected to form its membership. In 1911 Archer had been elected to the Institute because of his highly acclaimed translation of *El Cid* and his identity as an "elegant scholar" of Spanish literature and history. In 1921 he and his mother had financed the construction of an administration building on Audubon Terrace.[8] The next year Archer was elected to the Academy. This left the two intertwined insti-tutions still without an exhibition gallery and an auditorium. According to Anna, in the spring of 1928 Archer now wanted to finance a second building to fill these needs.

At last with Duveen's check for the *Aristotle* in his pocket he could begin. The building lot was to be 100′ x 100′ on the northwest corner of Audubon Ter-race opposite that built in 1923 on the southwest cor-ner. (D1928, October 11) Cost would be about $600,000, and Cass Gilbert would be the architect. To bring this plan about he had "railroaded" Nicholas Murray Butler, president of Columbia University, into the presidency of the Academy. (Anna does not explain how.) (D1928, October 26) Archer must have known he was treading unpre-dictable waters, for Butler had been hinting at the union of the Hispanic Society of America with Columbia. "This quite depressed Archer, as it would mean the ruin of the H.S.A. Columbia ruins every-thing it touches." (D1928, October 26) Anna was borrowing trouble, for this event never happened, and the second building was built and occupied by 1930.

* * *

MEANWHILE, Anna had recovered her strength. Rationing herself to a daily half-hour in her studio and gradually increasing her time there, she com-pleted the flagpole base for the *El Cid* ensemble. Her mother, now 88 years old, whom she had not seen for over a year and who lived in Princeton, New Jersey, came through New York on her way to the family farm at Annisquam on Cape Ann, Massachusetts. She stopped for lunch and a long visit. Another visi-tor was Carrie Campbell whom she took to the stu-dio to see *El Cid*. In fact, with many visitors passing through in the spring, Anna found it pleasant to entertain them at lunch and then have *El Cid* to look at afterwards.

Delighted to resume her role as sculptor, she got together 16 pieces of sculpture and took them to Roman Bronze, her foundry, located in Corona, N. Y., in Queens, to be cast. Her *Bulls Fighting*, on exhibit at the National Academy of Design, had been awarded the coveted Julia A. Shaw Memorial prize, which was for merit and must be given only to an American woman artist.[9] To see it again Archer and Anna went to 1083 Fifth Avenue, their former home, where the National Academy of Design was now ensconced.

With the weather in the high 80s, they were eager to depart for Camp Arbutus in the Adirondacks. But first, their car had to be delivered. "The car company sent up a Rolls-Royce instead of our usual Packard to try out. It would be $50 more a week. We tried it. It is more comfortable, less bumpy, but not as quiet. Also the Packard is made here. So Archer told the company he did not care for the Rolls." (D1928, June 3) In early August, in their quiet American car, they drove to Camp Arbutus for an invigorating five weeks. Temperatures were in the 70s, and they had no social obligations. On one of the last days Anna walked around the lake. "Found that 4 miles is too long; not that I felt in the least tired or too hot; but at night felt heart strain."

On return in September announcement was made that Archer had donated $100,000 for the development of American sculpture. This unsolicited gift went to the National Sculpture Society for arranging the largest exhibition of sculpture ever put on in the country. Its venue was to be the California Palace of the Legion of Honor in San Francisco. The intent was to show the spectrum of American sculpture, and no piece would be rejected for either academic or modernist tendencies. Enthusiastically received by sculptors everywhere, this was another Hyatt-Huntington cooperative plan, the first having been the exhibit set up by the National Sculpture Society on Audubon Terrace in the summer of 1923. A practicing sculptor's influence could be seen in what the *New York Times* called distributing the funds in the "most practical way, covering the artists' packing and shipping expenses."10

* * *

ENGAGEMENTS FOCUSING on matters Spanish dotted their autumn calendar. King Alfonso XIII, who was expecting to welcome Archer and Anna in Madrid in the spring of 1929, was enthusiastically promoting the building of an enlarged University of Madrid founded along U. S. lines. Sent by the King, Lucretia Bori, the Metropolitan Opera's popular prima donna, came to lunch at No. 1 to tell the Huntingtons about a benefit performance on November 15 of *La Traviata* to raise money for the university. She arrived a full half-hour early, and Anna found her charming and lively. The King couldn't have chosen a more effective emissary. At luncheon, Archer gave $5000 for a parterre box in the Diamond Horseshoe on that special night, and to endow a bed at the proposed university.

The performance was a highlight during the visit to New York of the Infante and the Infanta of Spain and their entourage. The Infante was Don Alfonso of Orleans, a first cousin of the King, and his wife, the Infanta Beatrix, was a sister of Queen Marie of Rumania; with them was their son, Prince Don Alvaro of Orleans and Bourbon, and the Marquis de Villaviejo and his daughter, Señorita Dona Pomposa de Escandon. "Tall, dark, and good-looking, very slender and a woman nearly 40," wrote Anna after she had been to a luncheon for the royal party on Park Avenue, "the Infanta has 3 grandsons. The Infante is good-looking too, and is interested only in aviation for which he was sent over. She is interested in everything and wants especially to see a large chicken farm. She delights in museums and could hardly be gotten away from the Hispanic where the party went after lunch . . . They all seemed to like my Cid very much which was a pleasure to me, as doing the heroes of another nation is rather uncertain if one is going to please the nation." (D1928, November 15)

During their visit to New York the royal party were guests of Brigadier General and Mrs. Cornelius

39

Vanderbilt III who lived at 640 Fifth Avenue in the huge brownstone palace built in 1880–1882 by his grandfather, William H. Vanderbilt. "Commodore" Cornelius Vanderbilt (1794–1877), who built up the tremendous family fortune was his great-grandfather. Situated at the northwest corner of Fifth Avenue and Fifty-first Street, the double four-story residence stood on a lot fronting 100 feet on the Avenue. William H. Vanderbilt had four sons and four daughters, and half of them lived on the west side of Fifth Avenue between Fifty-first and Fifty-seventh streets in palaces he had erected for them.

By 1930 the high winds of change were blowing strong. In 1927 the palaces of William K. Vanderbilt at Fifth Avenue and Fifty-second Street and that of Cornelius Vanderbilt II at Fifth and Fifty-seventh Street, both built around 1880, one after the other, were demolished and had to yield to fashionable shops like Bergdorf-Goodman, F.A.O. Schwartz, and Bonwit Teller.[11] (Arabella's palace at 2 East Fifty-seventh Street was demolished in the same year.) Only 640 Fifth Avenue escaped the wrecker's ball, and stood antiquated and massive, through the wartime period. (In 1947 the Crowell Publishing Co. bought and demolished it, then built their own building on the same lot.)[12]

When Grace and Cornelius Vanderbilt III moved into the W. H. Vanderbilt palace they became leaders of New York society. William H. had willed his residence to George W. Vanderbilt, his fourth son, who had lavished his inheritance on developing his Biltmore estate in Asheville, N.C. The 14th clause in the will specified that if George died without a male heir to carry on the Vanderbilt name, No. 640 should go to Cornelius III. George died in 1914 having sired

only a daughter, and Cornelius and Grace, his southern wife, had moved in.[13] Grace loved entertaining. Remodeling the residence, she made it the social center of the Avenue and Manhattan.

Her husband, who was known as "Neily," was, as Louis Auchincloss wrote, "a sober, serious man with a fine mind for engineering and locomotive design. Becoming a brigadier general, he served in France in the First World War." When the request came to house and entertain the Spanish royal party, he probably agreed with resignation. After all, "he was a Vanderbilt and had inherited his father's puritanical sense of duty."[14] This analysis may help us understand why he appeared to Anna as she described him at a luncheon she and Archer were invited to on November 16. Here is her account.

A lunch of nearly 50 mostly old friends of Archer's who seemed so glad to see him. The host looked and acted most awfully bored and stood off by himself—she is now quite stout, her face a frozen mask that almost never cracks to smile and her manner stiff as a ramrod. The house reflects this—very dark so you have to peer at people to know them, the room cold and formal with no personal touch, the service at table was like a hotel; the one thing necessary seemed to be hustle, the men almost throwing the plates on the table and three times there were crashes of dishes and many droppings of forks and hurried scanty courses that one's hunger could not be satisfied, the cooking not attractive—altogether a sloppy atmosphere.

After lunch we all stood on end in a room

with so few chairs that no one dared sit down and of course we could not as the Infanta and hostess stood; no one dared leave until old waddly Mrs. Whitelaw Reid started to say goodbye—then everyone followed with a rush—our hostess stood away from the crowd, away from the Infanta as if she was bored and irritated—between this restless woman and the host staring at the ground most of the time with a frown, the atmosphere was anything but pleasant.[15]

If Mr. and Mrs. C. Vanderbilt frowned, stared at the floor, and stood ramrod-stiff, they should not be criticized. The night before they had hosted a reception with dancing followed by a buffet supper for two hundred members of New York's most illustrious old families. And the evening before that they had filled several parterre boxes at the Metropolitan Opera for the special performance of *La Traviata*. No wonder when Anna returned to No. 1 she felt "tired from those two days and lay on the roof all the p.m."

* * *

BEFORE SAILING on December 21, Anna and Archer had much to do. At the Hispanic Society he spent several days working with electricians to adjust the lighting in a new wing. He even made an effective screen of cloth to hang and cut off the direct light so it reflected down on the paintings. He went to the dentist and the eye-man. Anna took her recently finished *Jaguars* to Berthold Nebel to be enlarged. She bought a new hat, had her first permanent hair wave, and decided to try a new gadget, "a savage vibrator" to reduce the flesh on her hips. They entertained twice at lunch and took friends to the Hispanic Society to see a display in the Sorolla room. This consisted of eighty drawings and models of the proposed university campus at Madrid. Archer was so busy that he didn't get to his lawyer's office to pick up their passports until a few days before departure.

Occupied up to the last minute, they went aboard at 8 p.m. "Poor Miss Perkins was nearly frantic with all the last minute instructions and broke into tears at our goodbyes." Once on board, they scanned the passenger list. Nobody they knew was on board. They didn't have to speak to anyone for ten entire days.

Three days before sailing they heard that "Helen G. B. and he (Granville Barker, the man for whom Helen had left Archer) are arriving on the *Olympic*, the steamer we intend leaving on. I am glad now we are going—it would not be agreeable to meet her." (D1928, December 18)

1. David B. Dearinger. *The Archer M. Huntington house at 1083 Fifth Avenue, New York.* National Academy of Design. 2002. 1.

2. Ibid., 7.

3. Ibid., 1.

4. Sheila M. Rothman. *Living in the Shadow of Death: Tuberculosis and the Social Experience of Death.* A Division of Harper, Collins Publishers, Inc. 1994. 2, 4, 6, 12.

5. Darwin Porter & Danforth Prince. *Frommer's Spain 2002.* Hungry Minds, Inc. New York, N.Y. 2002. 267.

6. Anthony Bailey. *Rembrandt's House.* Houghton, Mifflin Company, Boston. 1978. 171, 202.

7. Thorpe, 334.

8. Proske. 20.

9. *Bulls Fighting*, Proske, 10; Susan Harris Edwards. *Anna Hyatt Huntington, Sculptor and Patron of American Idealism.* Thesis submitted in partial fulfillment of the requirements for the Degree of Master of Arts, University of South Carolina. 1983. 24.

10. Cook, 10.

11. I. N. Phelps. *New York Past and Present 1524–1939.* 50. A guidebook to the World's Fair. 1939.

12. Ronda West. *On Fifth Avenue Then and Now.* Birch Lane Press. Carol Publishing Group. 1992. New York, N.Y. 169.

13. W. A. Croffut. *The Vanderbilts.* The Arno Press. New York, N.Y. 1975. 168, 224. This book is part of a series called, "The Leisure Class in America," published by Belford, Clarke & Company, Chicago and New York. 1886. The book contains the full text of William H. Vanderbilt's will.

14. Louis Auchincloss. *The Vanderbilt Era: Profiles of a Gilded Age.* New York. Charles Scribner's Sons. 1989. 114.

15. *New York Times*, 17 November 1928.

CHAPTER 4

ALGIERS, MOROCCO, SEVILLE, AND MADRID

1929

AFTER LANDING AT CHERBOURG, the Huntingtons drove through France to the Riviera, and then east to Genoa in Italy. On February 2 they boarded a Dutch steamer, the *Jan Pieterson Coon*, to travel down the Adriatic into the Mediterranean, bound for Algiers on the north African coast. It was Sunday, and the scene was the saloon where they were lunching at a table with three English people. Happy to be in a cosmopolitan atmosphere, with people who were well traveled and well read, they talked at length with a Dutch couple who had an interest in this line of Dutch steamers.

The Italian chef did not disappoint them. For dinner they had "Risotto rice and saffron—Ravioli pasta of macaroni stuffed with finely minced meat and green vegetables—Calomari devil fish—zabaglione well beaten eggs and hot white wine—" (No mention of a nap afterwards!) Docking at Algiers on Sunday and walking down the gangway, the Huntingtons were pleased that two of the gentlemen came to say goodbye and Godspeed. (D1929, February 2)

Anna and Archer's visit to the ancient port city lasted about three weeks. Cook's Travel had arranged a car and driver for them. At first they explored the fertile landscape along the Mediterranean. Then,

despite storm and rain and determined to see the sights, they drove up into the Maritime Atlas mountains, passing large fenced farms for Arab stallions, forests of cork oak trees, herds of sheep and goats and clusters of tents in an occasional oasis. Finally, they came to Biskra, their destination on the edge of the Sahara Desert , 150 miles south of Algiers. It was Ramadan, the Muslim Holy Week, and peering inside the huge mosque called Sidi Okba, they saw rows of men in white kaftans, each kneeling on his rug, murmuring a low monotone prayers; one fanatic frothed at the mouth.

Here, "an old roman bridge arched over a narrow valley with two red stone pillars that looked like giant towers of a ruined castle, all shining in the sun." (D1929, February 20) Archer did not get up on a camel, but Anna did because she never had. They drove along a rough high road at 3,000 feet above sea-level to Constantine, stopping at Setif to watch flocks of storks building nests in towers and trees. One rare day it was sunny, warm, and clear, and driving through the desert they saw a mirage that looked like a great blue sea. Everything was of interest to Anna and Archer—with one exception. When the driver suggested a public bath, recently built, artistically tiled, and with clean water—one side for men and the other for women—they balked. The Huntingtons preferred their own hotel-bath.

Unpleasant weather with heavy rainstorms and cold winds from the north made Anna dig into her trunk for leg-gaters and a blanket for Archer to keep their legs warm. This contrasty weather gave Archer a chest cold with low temperature, so they alternated sightseeing with rest-days in their suite to write letters and recover from indigestion caused by the strange Algerian cuisine.

But Anna had come well-prepared. If Archer felt feverish, she had what she needed in her medical kit—headache pills, a thermometer, and some physics. When his back grew sore and his feet ached from walking, especially the right big toe, Anna got out his larger shoes, which he had forgotten he had. Easier to walk in, he agreed to go out with her to have their fortunes told. Bored by the weather, the people and their dirty habits, and having exhausted what there was to do and see, they packed up seven trunks and sent them express to Gibraltar in care of Cook's; then headed for Oudja, 230 miles west over the border into Morocco. They met no other vehicle on the road. It was March 4. Three more weeks and they would be in Spain.

What would Morocco be like? In 1892 Archer had been there to study Arabic before translating *El Cid*. Anna had never been there. A detached observer, Anna seldom wrote how she felt, but this Islamic Kingdom must have inspired her—diary pages crowded to the edges with sentences written so close as to be legible only through a magnifying glass. Al-Masghreb al-Aqsa, the Farthest Land of the Setting Sun, as the ancient Arabs called it, lies due south of the Strait of Gibraltar. Facing toward the Atlantic Ocean, its southern periphery backs up into the snow-capped High Atlas mountains.

The Moors are a mix of Arabs, Spanish Muslims, and Berbers, a vigorous tribal people inhabiting the mountains. Everywhere they settled are distinguishing marks of their ingenious methods of garden irrigation, and architecture with arches shaped like horseshoes decorating arcades, doorways, patio walls. Yet it was not the history and architecture that excited Anna, but, rather, the people, how they lived, and the local daily scene.

After dropping their trunks at the hotel in Fez, Anna and Archer headed for the heart of the old city called the medina. Here the network of streets is so narrow and labyrinthine they had to abandon their car and ride on mules. "You look down a long dark passage to a blue-tiled doorway. Souks covered with lattice to screen them from the sun swarm with people, veiled women, children carrying baked bread always coughing or running at the nose, bear (sic) headed fanatics, fat well-dressed jews, laden donkeys, everybody yelling, bargaining, cursing . . . Each street has its own smell according to trade, street of carpenters smells of wood; another of spices, reeking of cayenne, saffron; another of leather-workers, of acid dye . . . a surging, milling crowd of brilliant color . . .

"There are so many mosques in Fez that the intervals in the evening prayer-call are most interesting in their choice of different wind instruments playing every tone from the nasal to the sonorous base; then there is pandemonium of reed instruments, bagpipes, drums, instruments that buzz like giant bees going all night for the 6 week festival of Ramadan . . . " (D1929, March 1–11)

44

Before leaving Fez for Marrakesh, they visited the Sultan's Palace where gardens, irrigation canals, fountains, and plantings combined to present a scene so memorable that Anna sketched the layout of the palace on the back page of her diary.

Archer continued to battle his chest cold so the couple bypassed Rabat and Meknes, to take refuge in what Anna called the "best hotel since leaving Menton." (This may have been *La Mamounia*, a five-star 'luxe' built between 1925 and 1929 for the French-controlled Moroccan railways.) Here in a comfortable suite Archer enjoyed attentions lavished on him by his wife; Anna was so concerned that he recover before departing for Spain that she scarcely went out herself. They did, however, exert themselves to stroll in the hotel's palm-shaded gardens where orange-blossoms gave off delicious aromas.

When Archer felt better they took a horse-carriage to the medina. This large plaza is dominated by the Koutoubia Mosque where, for centuries as the sun was setting over the Atlantic Ocean, farmers, traders, thieves, and food-venders, gathered to mill around. "We stopped to watch a snake-charmer who was prancing and foaming at the mouth about his snakes—he came to us with a large fat desert-snake that looked like a rattler—and held it up for us to stroke saying it was good luck—and then put it in my lap expecting me to be frightened and pay him to remove it. Archer said in Arabic—"No power nor strength but in God." The charmer and crowd were so delighted, the performer drew his snake away. (D1929, March 18)

A few days later, the couple made their journey across the Strait to Gibraltar. In Customs at the old British fortress, a "nice bobby said he'd hire Archer any day he spoke such good Spanish." (D1929, March 29)

Gathering up their trunks, they drove to Algeciras for the night. A message from the Marqués de Vega Inclán, their Spanish host, awaited them, saying he would see them the next morning. Archer said he was very, very happy to be in Spain again.

The next day, waiting for the Marqués, Anna and Archer indulged in a universal pastime: they bought candies. "Several sweet specialties, an almond paste, very nice; a fig sausage, not so good; almond drops like those at home; and sugar-coated pine nuts, not bad—pinoca." (D1929, March 30)

The Marqués arrived, "quite old-looking, surprisingly strong, animated and pleasant; speaks French almost as badly as I do, but more fluent, wears blue glasses. We started right away for Seville, passing rolling fields, fertile grain fields, orchards with olive and cork trees in neat rows. Immense pastures for sheep, cows, and fine, big, fat, black fighting bulls.

"Arrived in Seville about 5 p.m., and went immediately to see Cid—finely placed in a large square called Glorieta San Diego."[1]

The Glorieta (Spanish for "rotary") was the intersection of four major roads, and situated immediately in front of the entrance to the exposition, near the banks of the historic Guadalquivir River. Men were still painting pavilions and stretching tents over poles. From his perch high on his warhorse, El Cid looked up at the Hotel Alfonso XIII, recently finished to house dignitaries arriving for the fair. (Ornate and rococo in style, even today the guidebooks rate it four-star.) In another direction, Cid sees the big tobacco factory where Georges Bizet's flirtatious, black-eyed Carmen rolled cigarettes on her thigh

The first *El Cid* Anna Hyatt Huntington finished was sent to Seville in 1927 to celebrate the International Exposition set for the spring of 1929. It faces Maria Luisa Park and was the Huntingtons' gift to Spain. Credit, *L'œuvres d'Anna Hyatt Huntington* par Émile Schaub-Koch. Editions Messein. Paris. 1949. 8.

and caught the roving eye of the handsome torero, Escamillo. The old factory is now part of the University of Seville.

The capital of Andalusia, Seville is one of Spain's most romantic and beautiful cities. And during Anna and Archer's visit it was Holy Week, with processions of penitents carrying tall candles and slowly walking through the streets to the cathedral. It was also the season for orange groves in bloom, for flower-filled patios, and for gypsies dancing flamenco. The scene at the river's edge was equally lively. For centuries Seville has been a busy river port, fifty miles from the Mediterranean Sea. Ferdinand and Isabella held court there and, after Columbus showed what the New World could produce, its docks and wharves were where the fabled Spanish galleons tied up to funnel their gold and silver into wagons destined for the royal mints. Today, commercial vessels still dock there for cargo and passengers.

To welcome the Americans, Don Benigno had pulled out all the stops. In the next few days the governor of the province, the mayor of Seville, and the American ambassador called upon the Huntingtons. Before a crowd, the Municipal Council of Seville conferred on them the title of *Hijos Adoptivos*, citizens of the city.[2]

Anna and Archer were invited to bull fights. "We were in a great yellow ring, in the president's box, surrounded by a black-dressed crowd of 10,000. Bulls rushed in, some bold, some frightened, and then came padded horses carrying the toreadors. Padding was ineffective and some were disemboweled and others wounded where horns ripped their hind legs. Horses were terribly frightened, quivering and trembling. Toreadors stabbed the bull two, three times without killing. Bad work. A sickening sight, and also boring after the first bull." (D1929, March 31)

Before leaving, as if to wash the sight of the lacerated horses out of her mind, Anna had her hair dressed. One hopes the barber was named Figaro and that, as his scissors shaped her hair, she remembered that thirty years later, after Rossini wrote *The Barber*, Mozart staged his *Marriage* in the same charming city. (D1929, March 27)

By the middle of April, Anna and Archer were in Madrid. On reaching the Ritz Hotel, they found so many calls and invitations had rained down on them that Anna wrote, "Things are getting thick. Too many people wanting to see us." (D1929, April 9) This is not surprising when one considers the Huntingtons many artistic and cultural ties with the Spaniards developed over the years. Don Benigno, who was president of the Commission for Tourism, helped them with their scheduling.

Archer wanted to renew cherished associations, but he also had a specific plan in mind to accomplish during the visit—he wanted to collect as many portraits of eminent Spaniards in the form of busts or paintings as time and connections would allow. Accordingly, at his request, Don Benigno made their first engagement with, not the king, but the noted sculptor named Mariano Benlliure y Gil. Archer commissioned Benlliure to model a series of busts to be cast in bronze and delivered to the Hispanic Society. Eventually, models of three statesmen and of a much-beloved physician, arrived at the society. They were Count of Romanones, three times prime minister, the Marqués de Vega Inclán, Primo de Rivera, prime minister from 1923 to 1930, and Dr. Gregorio Marañón.

A close friend of the painter Joaquin Sorolla (1863–1923), who had created for the Society a stunning series of fourteen large paintings of the Spanish provinces, Benlliure took the Huntingtons to see the Casa de Sorolla. It was a poignant scene. The house had been left as it was when the artist died, unfinished canvas on the easel, the old hat on a hook, the palette knife, the little garden with spring flowers blooming. And Benlliure a fine guide. "He was most kind with his praise of Cid. I should say no jealousy. Took us to the Prado in the late afternoon when the light was soft and luminous on that magnificent collection." (D1929, April 19)

During the following week they were entertained at a series of sumptuous lunches, first at the Royal

Portrait of *Jacabo Fitz-James Stuart y Faleco, the seventeenth Duke of Alba*, by Fernando Alvarez de Sotomayor, 1929. Finished in time for the visit to Madrid of Archer and Anna Huntington in April 1929. It was shipped and presented to the Hispanic Society by the Duke.

Palace with King Alfonso who wanted to talk about the future university; then successively, lunches with the prince of Asturias (title for the heir apparent), the American ambassador and his wife (Mr. and Mrs. Hammond) at the embassy, the count of Aguilar, and the seventeenth duke of Alba. The latter was pleased when Anna said she would put his head on one of the figures in a mural at the society. He sent for photos, and ordered his portrait shipped to the Hispanic Society. The artist, Fernando Alvares de Sotomayor, had just finished painting it.

In addition, the duke invited the Huntingtons to watch his induction into the mediaeval Order of Santiago in the chapel of that name. Seated in the back with the duke's family, they saw him enter, dressed in military uniform, walk down the aisle between knights dressed in black and wearing hats trimmed with ostrich plumes, and kneel before the head knight. The sword was passed over his head and shoulders. Rising, the duke then walked down the aisle, between the knights, embracing each of the 130 men in turn.

Before departing, Archer had to decide what to do with the gifts that had been showered on them during their stay. The Tourism Commission questioned his taking them out of the country. Archer did not want to offend anyone, but he finally told Don Benigno that the situation was absurd. "Leave them here," he said. Anna, however, refused to leave her gift—Count Aguilar gave her twelve boxes of perfume "because I said I had none." (D1929, April 17)

Don Benigno invited them to spend the last night with him. Although tired, they could not refuse him. After supper he took them upstairs to their room. Wishing them a good sleep, he told Archer that Spanish carpenters do not count on people being so tall. "You may have to wrap your long legs around the railing," he suggested, "or even sleep doubled up, knees to your chest." Laughing, Archer said he was so tired he could sleep in any position. After he went downstairs, Don Benigno heard a resounding crash. Alarmed, he rushed up to find Anna laughing and helping Archer struggle to his feet out of the ruins of his bed. "It looks like you will have to spend the night on the floor, Don Archer." Amused by his predicament, Archer did just that with a few pillows to soften his position. The next morning he told the Marqués he had actually slept quite well.[3]

On April 19, by 9:30 a.m., the Huntingtons were off and away, driving through Vallalodid, Burgos, and the Pyrenees to Biarritz in France. "We slept like the dead all night," wrote Anna. Arriving in Paris, Archer collapsed with laryngitis and a cold in his lungs. Anna nursed him with hot packs, hot drinks, gargles, and prescriptions from the hotel doctor. Too sick to go out, he asked Anna to arrange for their return voyage. She obtained a small suite on the *Statendam* of the Holland-American line, sailing May 6. Archer soon rallied and enjoyed the trip through Belgium to Rotterdam where the *Statendam* awaited them.

When they arrived at New York, Annie, their housekeeper at No. 1, met them. Archer was off to the Hispanic Society and when he returned, he told Anna all that had happened in their absence.

---

1. Darwin Porter & Danforth Prince. *Frommer's Spain 2002.* Hungry Minds, Inc. 2002. An excellent map of Seville is on p. 267. The Glorieta where *El Cid* stands is called Glorieta San Diego. The tobacco factory where Carmen worked is on Calle de San Fernando, near the Glorieta San Diego.

2. *The History of the Hispanic Society of America.* Written by the staff. Published by the Hispanic Society of America. 1954. 8. This book celebrates the Hispanic Society's Fiftieth Anniversary.

3. G-M, 467.

CHAPTER 5

"A QUIET JOINING OF HANDS BETWEEN SCIENCE AND ART"

1929–1931

IN THE SUMMER OF 1929 a felicitous event took place that eventually altered the course of the Huntingtons' lives. "It was a Sunday morning in Uncle Archer's Fifth Avenue home," recalled Brantz Mayor, Anna's nephew who had just been graduated from Princeton and was visiting at 1083 while looking for a job. "The livingroom was one flight up for a better view of Central Park. Sunlight flooded the room. He was in conference. Soon the doubledoors to the diningroom opened and out trooped eight to ten gloomy big shots followed by Uncle Archer who in contrast was radiant with pleasure. After they left he explained that he had called the meeting of top bankers and brokers to coordinate his instructions to sell every share of common stock that he owned with minimal effect on the stock market. This was probably in large part his inheritance from his mother. The reason he was taking such drastic action, was because of his shock upon returning from Spain, to find his common stock portfolio had increased in value beyond all reason. The situation was unsound, so he would have none of it. Not one of the big shots had agreed with his action. But to him this only confirmed that he was right."[1]

Then laughing, Brantz told how Archer gave vent to his exuberance. "He and I got talking about boxing and the effectiveness of a short jab. I questioned his emphasis. So he asked me to make a fist and hold it against my chest. He then put his fist one fist away from my chest, warned me to tense up and then hit me. I went spinning across the livingroom, caught my heel on a footstool, and ended up flat on a bear rug in front of the fireplace. Aunt Anna shouted, 'Archer!' I was tough as a boot and not even shaken up but convinced about the effects of a short infighting jab. So we all had a good laugh and went to lunch."[2]

When elated and feeling his oats, Archer's knee-jerk reaction was to found a museum or plan a trip. This time was no exception. On that fatal Tuesday, the very day the stock market crashed, he told Anna he had a scheme to found a Mariners' Museum at the Newport News Shipbuilding and Drydock Company, which he and his California family owned. Homer Ferguson, the general manager, had come for lunch and shared his enthusiasm. (D1929, October 29) The plan was put on the backburner, but not for long.

About this same time, there arrived in the mail an intriguing travel brochure. It described a large tract for sale near Georgetown, South Carolina, entitled "Four Colonial Plantations on the Waccamaw River."[3] Considering this, Archer and Anna realized coastal South Carolina offered possibilities, a new venue and temperate climate in which Anna might better recover from her persistent illness. Although far from well, she had times of remission such as during the recent journey abroad, that encouraged her to resume her former creative, energetic life. But inevitably, the symptoms would return, the bronchial cough, the daily temperatures, the blood in the sputum, then the frustrating need to rest. Camp Arbutus in the Adirondacks had been a partial solution; the altitude there was high, the air cold and dry. But access to it was circuitous and subject to sudden snowstorms. Moreover, housekeeping drained Anna's energies. In essence, Camp Arbutus had lost its attraction. In South Carolina there would be no social obligations as there were in New York. In November and December, for instance, the Huntingtons had entertained 165 people for lunch or dinner. "Tired," wrote Anna in her diary. (D1929, December 6) This was unlike her. She scarcely ever complained. But the account of old derelict plantations, migrating birds on the marshes, the grassy savannas alternating with stands of cypress, saltwater inlets and beaches, made her as eager as Archer to see a place so unlike New York.

In January 1930, Anna and Archer sailed down the Inland Passage to Georgetown, South Carolina, to visit the Four Colonial Plantations. When they arrived an agent told them all about the tract. Situated on Waccamaw Neck and bounded on the west

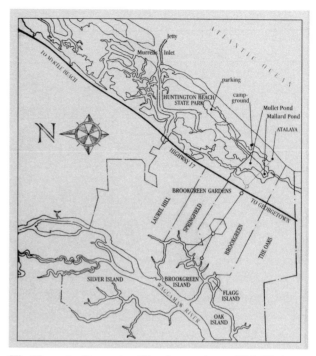

The Plantation Properties of Brookgreen. Across U.S. Highway 17 is the Huntington Beach State Park where Atalaya, once the Huntingtons' winter residence, is located. In March 1941, the Huntingtons deeded Atalaya and surrounding property to Brookgreen Gardens. In 1960 the State of South Carolina signed a fifty-year lease agreement with Brookgreen Gardens for 2500 acres of ocean front property on which to create a state park. Credit, *Visitor's Guide.* Published 2001. South Carolina State Park Service. 91.

by the Waccamaw River and on the east by the Atlantic Ocean, it was composed of four rundown plantations named (starting from the northernmost): Laurel Hill, Springfield, Brookgreen, and The Oaks. Altogether they comprised 6,635 acres, and were collectively called "Brookgreen," after the most historic of the four and the one with the best beach on the ocean.

The original owner of Brookgreen, John Alston, had had a royal grant for the property. One of his descendants, Theodosia Burr Alston, only daughter of Aaron Burr, was plantation mistress in the early 1800s. Prior to the Civil War the plantation had grown rice and indigo, and had prospered. In the late 1860s, when farmhands migrated north after emancipation, the owners turned to raising cotton, a crop needing less labor.

In 1920 Willie and Julia Peterkin were the owners of Brookgreen Plantation; it was the year the vicious boll weevil had reached low-country, South Carolina. (Julia made literary history in the twenties by publishing three novels; one of these, *Scarlet Sister Mary*, a story about the Negroes who lived on Brookgreen Plantation, won a Pulitzer Prize.) Hoping to salvage his crop, Willie laid in a supply of calcium arsenate and bought expensive equipment to spread it. But the farmhands balked at handling the green dust: "When de cotton is wet wid dew," they said, "a pizen dust'll stick to yo' feet."[4]

Faced with bankruptcy, the Peterkins sought help from Julia's father, Dr. Julius Mood, a prosperous doctor in Sumter, South Carolina. He formed a partnership to buy the huge tract and use it as a shooting preserve. But when hard times struck, the partners were forced to turn it over to the F. M. Credit Corporation, which in 1930 was liquidating its South Carolina properties.

Its romantic but unfortunate history only rendered the place more attractive to Anna and Archer who welcomed a challenge to restore prosperity and glory to any derelict, once-thriving old property. "I must tell you about our day at Brookgreen," wrote Anna to a friend. "Most of the inhabitants seemed to have the leisure to watch us land at Georgetown—a small sleepy town. Our captain took pains to move as slowly as possible. I feel like I'm taking part in a comic play when we step across the gangway with the steward and officers all at attention." After describing a low Japonica in bloom and ancient box hedges overgrown with vines, Anna said she felt a strong impulse to sit on the porch and not go back on the boat. "The house on the beach is quite different. Built almost on the sand with no trees or bushes in sight—also small and primitive—tho' not old and only heated by fireplaces. It's probably only cold at night and we can manage this year, adding on later."[5]

The Huntingtons hired a driver and car and explored Brookgreen. The former two-story gun-club house had two chimneys at either end of a steep pitched roof; its three gables, and long low architecture had a colonial feel to it and smacked of New England. Anna liked its simplicity. In fact, she wrote in her diary, "All we need are two chairs, a table and some books, and we could move right into it." (D1930, March 2)

The place appealed to Archer for different reasons. He noticed how rundown Brookgreen looked, how poor and uneducated the Negroes were who lived in scattered, ramshackle houses made of boards on the Neck or on Sandy Island in the middle of Waccamaw. The strong humanitarian strain in his nature made him want to help these people. The plantation was a place the Huntingtons could restore by hiring a population in need of work. Archer liked start-ups; he was particularly drawn to troubled situations which he could improve by using his imagination, talents, and resources.

"There is certainly an enormous amount to be

done in draining, fencing and planting," wrote Anna. "We went over to see the Laurel Hill part that is on a bluff at the bend of a river (the Waccamaw)—most forlorn half hidden by wild growths, the river seen only from the bank, but it was a pretty view even in winter; in the distance one sees the tall brick chimney of the old rice-mill, only thing left. The former house is in ruins . . . I feel quite sure that the beach house to live in and the woods to ride in are all that we shall want. The white sand-paths that run among the trees shining like patches of snow among the yellow and green moss add to the lure. Even the swampland is lovely . . ." (D1930, March 29)

Archer, who, when in Spain, had observed how successfully the Moors irrigated their gardens, was already forming a vision of what could be done with the landscape. And he noticed a site on the dunes where a winter residence could be built. And here, at Brookgreen, they could design a garden-setting in the woods and swampland which would provide a background for Anna's sculpture.

So, Archer and Anna bought the property for $225,000 on January 24, 1930. Later, as the idea of creating a wildlife preserve seeded itself in their imaginations, Archer bought 3,400 acres more to the north to provide migrating water-birds and coastal animals an inviolate refuge. Creating what evolved into Brookgreen Gardens was the first major project the couple embarked on together.

In March, they set up housekeeping in the beach house while planning how to develop the property. Even the arrival of Miss Perkins, Archer's secretary, with seven bags of mail didn't dampen their enthusiasm for their new lifestyle. Anna found a "creekboy" who brought them shrimp and oysters dug up at low

When at Camp Arbutus in the Adirondacks or even in the countryside around Atalaya, Archer enjoyed wielding an axe to test his strength. Courtesy, Anna Hyatt Huntington Papers, Syracuse University Library, Special Collections.

tide. "The delicious smell of pitch pine combines to give us fierce appetites for crabs and clams." (D1930, March 9)

Archer was enjoying not only the fresh shellfish, but also the pleasant sense of owning land and interacting with it. Hyatt Mayor remembered an incident that illustrates this. "In late March a prominent New York lawyer who was descended from the colonial rice planters of Brookgreen wanted to show his friend Bernard Baruch, a financier and presidential adviser, his ancestral domain. They pushed their way through the scrub and marshy growth, without finding anyone to ask permission to trespass. At last the sound of the crack of logs being split caught their attention, and they came upon a giant in bluejeans swinging an axe. They asked him if he thought the new owner would object to their trespassing. Uncle Archer had to admit he was the new owner. He then showed them around and charmed them with his hopes and dreams."[6]

Archer felt the itch to build. The close seawall reminded him of a fortress he had once seen on the south coast of Spain overlooking the Mediterranean Sea. He also remembered a watch-tower on the coast in Marrakesh, Morocco, used by the natives to spot Barbary pirate ships. "We must build a tower here," he told Anna. A population of bats skimming over-head and snatching bugs as they flew, prompted him to say: "We need that tower. I want to make a place for bats to roost and breed. In San Marcos, Texas south of Austin where I grew up they built towers to attract bats and exterminate the malarial mosqui-toes." (D1931, January 2)

There was a lot to do. Archer engaged a local con-tractor, William Thompson, and told him to hire 100 Negroes and start them cleaning up the garden area. The Depression had hit the region hard; the men had no work so families were living off the land and the tides. As descendants of slaves, the natives were illiterate, speaking a creole dialect called Gul-lah that made finding work elsewhere impossible. By hiring these men to construct the house and gardens, Archer offered them the opportunity to learn ma-sonry, plastering, and carpentry skills.

By May, the weather grew hot enough to force the Huntingtons to return to New York until January of the following year. But in their absence, a new con-crete roadway was built across a causeway to connect what became the Brookgreen Gardens with the area where the beach house was. Now the labor force and supplies could easily reach the site. Electricity run-ning from Georgetown to Brookgreen had been installed. Thompson was there every day to super-vise. And, upon his return, Archer, trim and tall in knickers and a cap, would meet with his manager daily to tell him what he wanted. Archer's plan, which as it took shape bore no resemblance to regional architecture, was not on paper but in his mind. Sometimes Archer's directions confused Thompson. "Mr. Huntington," he said, "if you tell me much more, I'll find out what you are building."[7]

Both the tower and U-shaped, one-story house he had in mind were to be made of brick. The buildings must be fireproof. Archer's fear of fire had its origin in a family catastrophe. On April 18, 1906, in the afternoon, a city-wide fire destroyed Collis Hunting-ton's house in San Francisco at 1020 California Street. His widow, Arabella, who was living there then, escaped. Four valuable paintings were cut out of their frames and saved from the fire, but nothing else. Although he was not there, the event made a lasting impression on Archer. Afterwards, everything he built had to be fireproof.[8] So Archer ordered two million bricks, that were delivered and dumped out-side the south walls. The masons laid concrete foun-dations and started constructing what was to be named "Atalaya," a Spanish word meaning watch-tower.

As the men hauled bricks to where the masons worked, Anna noticed some were so weak they couldn't even lift a shovel. Noticing, too, Archer sent for 35 strips of bacon, 70 lbs of coffee and sugar, 1 pail of candy, and doled out the food. Five families got $5 apiece for the time-being, and single men got $1 each. He also noticed one man who was barefoot because he owned no shoes. When Archer found out

Aerial View of Atalaya in the mid-century. Anna and Archer's suite was in the lower left corner. Courtesy, South Carolina Department of Parks, Recreation & Tourism.

LEFT: Atalaya today. Credit, Paul Hoffmann. RIGHT: The water tower of Moorish design in the center courtyard. Its design was inspired by Archer's memory of such a tower on the south coast of Spain built to watch for Barbary pirates. Credit, Paul Hoffmann.

he wore the same size shoe, size 14, he gave the fellow two pairs of his own shoes. (D1931, November 28; December 22) His concern for their welfare so touched the men that they worked on New Year's Day even though it was a holiday.

Soon Archer swung into action with a master plan for a Negro village. Hiring still another crew, he had a medical clinic built with an X-ray machine and staffed it with a dentist and physician; then two schools, a chapel, and the first paved road in Georgetown County. Small brick cabins were constructed with five rooms, a chimney in the middle, a kitchen, an ell with pump and a large tub, and a privy in the rear. Keeping track of the labor-force, their pay, and if they earned it, was a burdensome job. But the natives respected him, for they realized he was teaching them lucrative skills. (D1932, April 8)

Unable to work in the studio, Anna occupied herself with watching the construction of the tower and the house, and designed grilles for the windows and ironwork for the doorways. She wrote her diary and helped Archer with his correspondence. While resting, her mind was anything but idle. Lying on her bed she would bring up images in her mind for future sculpture. "Reminders: stallion; 3 colts playing, nicking and biting each other; coiled snake for a doorstop; seal scratching head with flipper; deerhound sitting mouth open and stag dead at feet; great dane." (D1931, December 22) Receiving her Charleston doctor's permission to model a small piece, Anna began a diamond-back terrapin. It was the first modeling she had down in two years. But the exertion was too much. The bronchial cough and the temperature of 99 to 100 returned, and she had to stop.

Despite setbacks, and impatient at being so unpro-

Anna's design for the entrance gate. Still sick with TB she couldn't exercise, but enjoyed designing window-grilles, gates, and hardware to embellish the austere brick walls of Atalaya. Credit, A. S. Goodrich.

ductive, on May 15, 1932, Anna drew a plan for the inside walls of the garden that Archer liked. Both were surprised to realize it took the shape of a butterfly with wings to either side. She said that inside the wings would be flowers like an old-fashioned garden, and outside, would be wild flowers. But doing this brought on a temperature, making Anna dizzy.

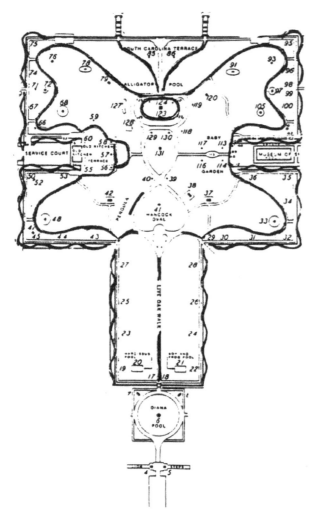

This is the first *Design for the Brookgreen Gardens* sketched by Anna, May 15, 1932. Her original sketch was not available to us. The photograph was copied with Susan Edwards' permission from her thesis submitted in partial fulfillment of the Masters of Art degree to the Art Department of the University of South Carolina. The thesis was entitled: "*Anna Hyatt Huntington: Sculptor and Patron of American Idealism.*"

Again, she had to stop. However, the crucial beginning had been made. The butterfly remains the basic design for today's spectacular gardens. (D1932, May 15)

The gardens presented engineering challenges—there must be water, and its flow through the gardens regulated. Many years later in 1949 in a talk to the American Institute of Decorators, Anna recalled:

I cannot take credit for the creation of Brookgreen Gardens, I am only the collaborator. My husband Archer Huntington created the garden. He planned it, drew it out, designed the curving openwork brick walls, the buildings. He laid out the central pool that supplies water for the irrigation and laid out a system of irrigating ditches after the Arabic system. The water flowed entirely by gravity and supplied as well all the pools about the statues. He used native labor entirely, teaching the brick layers how to lay foundations for the curving walls as well as how to build an arch of brick. Also the residence and openwork brick tower on the beach were built entirely under his direction.[9]

Noticing how well the lush foliage set off Anna's sculptures, they decided Brookgreen could become a veritable outdoor museum for the best contemporary American sculpture. The Huntingtons invited other sculptors to submit their work. And to ensure its future, Archer had his New York lawyer come to draw up papers that would establish Brookgreen Gardens with a Trust and Trustees as a "Society for Southeastern Flora and Fauna." At this same time, he also established the Mariners' Park in Newport News, Virginia, whose museum construction was about to begin. As he signed the deeds for establishing Brookgreen Gardens in 1931, Archer said, "The place will be a quiet joining of hands between science and art." (D1931, June 15)

At home in New York in 1932, Anna had a heartwarming surprise. Dean Charles W. Flint, Chancellor of Syracuse University came to tell her that the university wanted to bestow on her a degree of Doctor of Fine Arts and would come to her home to do it. This was a special honor since the university did not bestow degrees in absentia. The invitation had been extended twice before, but Anna was too ill to travel to the University to accept it. So, on the first of July Dean Flint arrived at 1083 with four other officials.

"Five professors came to lunch," wrote Anna. "Then all filed up to my sittingroom, and I felt very small and scared surrounded by five big men in solemn cap and gown. One read the citation of my election; another read the reasons for choosing me; a third placed the hood of orange and brown over my head. It was a trying and moving ordeal, and I feared I would weep. They also seemed moved, as two of them had tears in their eyes. We shook hands, welcoming me into the fraternity. Afterwards, Archer took them all to the Hispanic Society and the other buildings in the block. They were dead beat and came back for restoring drinks." (D1932, July 7)

Anna received another signal honor in 1932. On October 29 she was elected a member of the American Academy of Arts and Letters, the second woman to be elected to this prestigious institution. (D1932, October 29) The first was Julia Ward Howe for her "Battle Hymn of the Republic," who was elected in 1908 when she was 89 years of age.

Pleased by the recognition of his wife's achievements, Archer made a sudden decision. He would give the land surrounding Camp Arbutus to Syracuse University as a wildlife refuge, some 13,000 acres. The concept of creating a chain of such preserves for migrating birds had come to him when visiting the Mariners' Museum site in Newport News. Flocks of ducks were using its lake as a nesting haven. At Brookgreen he had seen the same stirring sight. Now a third refuge could be the woods and lakes in the Adirondacks near Camp Arbutus. On July 28 Archer had his lawyer draw up the deed transferring to Syracuse University the property except for Arbutus Lake and his camp's immediate surroundings. "All done," wrote Anna. "We were delighted." (D1932, July 28)

Eventually, this gift inspired Archer to donate his father's Camp Pine Knot at Raquette Lake, which he had inherited, as a second ecological center in the Adirondacks. This time, however, the recipient was State University of New York. The stories of both camps can be found as Appendices.

1. Brantz Mayer. "Uncle Archer." 5f.

2. David B. Dearinger. *The Archer M. Huntington House at 1083 Fifth Avenue*. The National Academy of Design. 2002. 1. José López Mezquita painted Archer Huntington's portrait in 1926. According to Mr. Dearinger, Mr. Huntington posed in the large "Salon" on the second floor of 1083. (David B. Dearinger to MM 4 June 2003.)

3. "Four Colonial Plantations on the Waccamaw River." Travel brochure found in *General Correspondence*. Series I, Box I. AHH Papers.

4. Susan Millar Williams. *Lives of Julia Peterkin*. University of Georgia Press. 1997. 24. Julia Peterkin once owned and lived on the Brookgreen Plantation.

5. Anna Hyatt Huntington to friend, January 29, 1930. *Visitor's Guide: Huntington Beach State Park*, South Carolina State Park Service, p. 7–8.

6. A. Hyatt Mayor, *Century*, p. 28.

7. *Visitor's Guide*. 12.

8. Dan Lewis to MM. 14 November 2001.

9. AHH to Karl Bock. 10 January 1949. *General Correspondence*, AHH Papers.

CHAPTER 6

FROM LEYSIN, SWITZERLAND, TO TUCSON, ARIZONA

1932–1934

· PART ONE ·

WITH ANNA STILL PRONE to temperatures, coughing and bleeding lungs, they decided to give up the usual winter stay at Brookgreen this year and, instead, seek out a first-class tubercular sanatorium where she would stay until she was cured. They chose one at Leysin, Switzerland, where Ada Marshall Johnson, the curator of silverwork at the Hispanic Society, had had a successful cure. It was also a place their New York physician had recommended. Southeast of Montreux, near the east end of Lake Geneva, the mountain village of Leysin was surrounded by peaks rising to over 10,000 feet. Here they stayed from August 18, 1932, to September 1933.

Below the huge sprawling sanatorium on the mountainside was a veritable village of chalets with balconies all facing south. Archer rented one called "La Pyrole." Here they put up bird-feeding boxes, and Archer threw meat to the birds, amusing the village children who gathered around on weekends to watch. The sound of cowbells so charmed Anna she had a box full of them shipped to No. 3 East Eighty-ninth Street in New York. Geisha, Anna's greyhound,

was with them, and also a toy French bulldog which Archer had spotted in a pet shop in Lausanne and couldn't resist bringing back to the chalet. He named her Cleo. "The whole household loves her," Anna wrote Miss Perkins. "Since I'm in bed all day, my nurse takes Geisha out, and Archer walks Cleo."[1]

A pleasant, relaxed pattern for living developed. Archer read French books to Anna in the evening. Often during the week, he went into Montreux to pick up mail. He would also bring back canned vegetables and fruit to vary their menu. Every morning he cut up oranges for Anna, arranging the pieces each time in varied patterns.

News from the States provided much to talk about. Syracuse University reported putting up notices that the tract the Huntingtons had given was now a Game Refuge in the name of Anna and Archer Huntington. An unexpected dividend of $700,000 came from the Newport News Shipyard, and they enjoyed discussing how to spend it.

While in the States, Archer had not paid attention to the financial news. But here, in Switzerland, he kept sharp track of it. The Depression was taking its

The letterhead for stationery of the Grand Hotel at Leysin, Switzerland, Anna's sanatorium for tuberculosis patients. She and Archer occupied a chalet called "La Pyrole" on the lower mountainside below the Hotel.

toll. "Out of 600 so-called millionaires in New York City," reported Archer, "only 65 are left. Nearly all are bankrupt." (D1933, January 1) The newly elected Democratic president, Franklin Delano Roosevelt, had closed the banks on Monday, March 6, and local Swiss banks refused to honor Archer's Letter of Credit. On March 10th, with Anna still mostly in bed and to cheer themselves up after such upsetting news, they celebrated their tenth anniversary with a cake and ten candles Archer had arranged for. "And people said they thought we'd only last two years," commented Anna. (D1933, March 10) Then like a belated birthday present, came the glorious news from the bank in Montreux, that New York City banks had reopened on March 14. It was a great relief.

Concerned that Archer was paying too much attention to her and not enough time pursuing his own pleasures, Anna suggested he go to Paris. He had been working hard on his poetry, and a French magazine in Paris had invited him to visit their offices. "They feel they are discovering a new voice in poetry," said Archer, laughing, but secretly pleased. "They want our photographs and ten pages of poems." When he returned he brought the decoration he received in 1927 when elected a Chevalier of the Legion of Honor. He had forgotten all about it. "All Paris is laughing at me." (D1933, March 10) He also brought Anna's decoration of "Officier" from the French Government, recognizing her gift of the monumental equestrian statue of Joan d'Arc placed on Riverside Drive in New York in 1915. The decoration was a cross, an unusual distinction since the French government itself had presented it and only four other women had been given the office. "One generally has to buy it," said Anna, down-playing the coveted honor. "A tiny jewelled cross that one wears on dress occasions." (D1933, March 10)

Gradually, week by week, Anna's health improved. Doctors came every day to monitor her temperature, tap her lungs. A van took her to the sanatorium for weekly lung X-rays. In ten months she had progressed from bedrest and balcony-siesta (wrapped like a mummy in blankets), to short walks only in fair weather, to being told that she could be out all day in any weather. She followed directions explicitly.

On September 7, 1933, came the long-awaited discharge. She was "cured." Accompanied by thirteen trunks, Anna and Archer left Leysin to stay at the Grand Hotel in Bellevue at Lago Maggiore in northern Italy for a month. After a year living at an altitude of 14,000 feet they needed to become accustomed to the lower altitude. "It made us all sleepy and lazy. Even Geisha wanted to sleep all the time." (D1933, September 7) Finally, on October 5, they sailed from Genoa on the Italian liner, *Rex*, and arrived in New York a week later. Miss Perkins met them at the dock.

In their absence this faithful, longtime secretary had become the clearinghouse for all kinds of errands and domestic cares. She took care of insurance payments, mail, employees' payroll, hiring staff for their New York home at No. 1 and No. 3 East Eighty-ninth Street. She had ordered Archer's tailor to make four coat-and-knicker suits for him from the four samples of tweed Anna had sent to her to be ready on return. She had even sent the Huntingtons toothpaste and boric acid ointment which they could not find in Leysin. Most important, in Anna's view, was preparing a room where Geisha could meet the puppies born to the greyhound bitch and left behind a year ago. "She must meet them, one at a time, so they will be friends," ordered Anna.[2]

· PART TWO ·

IT IS UNCLEAR how, when he was in Switzerland, Archer heard about an estate of 420 acres called Rocas (Spanish for "rocks") for sale at Haverstraw, New York. Built in the mid-twenties by a movie mogul named Sam Katz, it had a large, baronial stone house looking down onto the Hudson River, and was only thirty miles north of New York City. Come the Depression, Katz went bankrupt, and had to leave, carrying only what he could pack into a suitcase. Wanting to have a country place ready for Anna when they returned from Leysin, Archer bought Rocas, sight unseen, on October 16, 1933, for $260,000. He had an agent hire local people for staff, a handyman, gardeners, a caretaker, and housekeeper.

On their return to New York he told Anna about it. She was delighted. Archer then admitted he had thought of himself, too. He was looking forward to having time in the new home for meditation, writing poetry or a book, and soothing the arthritis stealing like a thief into his bones. Here they would be close to New York and the Hispanic Society, yet far enough away to discourage visitors. Anna didn't care for living in the city either. As long as she had a studio, she said she could adjust to anything. They soon moved out to Rocas and to Anna's relief, found the place totally furnished with all necessary linens, a well-equipped kitchen, and a wonderful spacious studio facing north.

But unfortunately, Anna was not able to resume her former design for living, for the tubercular symptoms returned, and her doctor advised a few months in Tucson, Arizona, to complete the cure. And so, late in November, the Huntingtons boarded a train for Tucson. Would she ever get over "this awful hanging about more dead than alive," she wondered, marveling at Archer's patience. "Not a murmur of protest, ever." (D1933, November 13)

In Tucson, they rented two houses, next to each other, one for themselves and the other for the staff they had brought—cook, chauffeur, and maid. Miss Perkins was ordered "to pack trunks with 2 doz. Sheets, 1 doz. Pillow-cases, 16 bath towels, and tablecloths from the Katz pantry, flat silver for 4 people; also to send 3 more suits for Archer, with long trousers, all grey if possible, and a stocking stretcher." (D1933, December 6) Annie, their faithful housekeeper from No. 1, came to Tucson bringing the linens and clothes. For four months Anna and Archer were comfortable and happy in the clear, dry

The main wing of "Rocas," where the Huntingtons lived from 1934 to 1940.

Arizona climate. Cecelia Beaux, a renowned portrait painter whom Anna knew, was taking the cure in a sanatorium nearby. Through her they met other artists. Socially, they enjoyed the winter but were glad to leave in early April with Anna in tip-top health, completely cured.

If she was disappointed to discover that Archer had planned their itinerary to drive through Texas, then to Pensacola, Savannah, to Brookgreen for the month of May, before returning to New York, Anna didn't mention it in the diary. Driving past San Anto-

nio, Archer said, "All through here as a boy I lived from 6 to 15 with my grandmother Yarrington on their ranch near San Marcos on the road to Austin." (D1934, March 17) Another stop was Newport News, Virginia, where Archer wanted to see how the Golf Museum at Newport News was coming along.

Yes, a golf museum. In 1931, while at Brookgreen, he had been at the shipbuilding yards in Newport News, and found out that some of the executives there were interested in forming a golf museum at the new James River Country Club. "I'm not much

62

One of two bronze lions Anna created for the gates into Brookgreen Gardens. One sphere shows the American side of the hemisphere, the other, the Far Eastern regions. Credit, Paul Hoffmann.

of a golfer," he had told them. "But if you people want a museum, I'll be glad to endow one for your clubhouse."[3] As was his way, Archer not only donated the seed-money to start construction. He also sent his plant engineer, Mr. John Campbell, to Europe with a pocketful of money to collect every golf relic available. Highlights of the collection were 150 balls dating from 1790 to 1932 and three clubs used by Bobby Jones in his championship years, including the Grand Slam, 1930. This happened before anyone thought of collecting golf artifacts,

and it was during the Depression, when you could get a lot for a little.[4] So this was how the oldest golf museum in America was started here at Newport News, Virginia. Now over seventy years old, it is still going strong.

Happy to be back at Brookgreen, Anna went to the beach house and unpacked boxes that hadn't been opened since she was there two years ago. Six large statues were set out on the grounds and looked surprisingly well. "These are not enough. We must get some more," she said. (D1934, March, 24) She was pleased, however, to see how well the main entrance looked with the two heraldic bronze lions on either side sitting back on their haunches. They had been designed, cast, and placed before she and Archer left for Switzerland. While at Atalaya she had made a quick study of her pet greyhound, Echo. "Did it in exactly 1 hr and 15 min from start to finish, and mostly from memory as she only lay in the same position once. I wanted to see if I still had my old eye and the quickness of hand I used to have." (D1935, January 30) Anna had not modeled a piece of sculpture for some six years. Finding out that her eye-hand coordination had not atrophied, she was elated.

Once at Rocas in early June, she wasn't there five days before putting on her smock, taking wire tool in one hand and a lump of clay in the other, and modeling marsh birds.

Archer had come to a decision, too. In June of 1934, realizing they no longer needed Camp Arbutus, on June 5, 1934, he deeded it and its surroundings to Syracuse University, rounding out their gift made two years before. He wanted to begin shedding responsibilities. The camp's maintenance had been a longtime burden, and he was glad to get rid of it.

1. AHH to Miss Perkins. 9 November 1932. Series 1. Box 12. *Correspondence*. AHH Papers.

2. AHH to Miss Perkins. 13 November 1933. Series I. Box 12. *Correspondence*. AHH Papers.

3. "World Class Golf. Old World Charm.—A Must-See Attraction." Christian Moody. *Virginia Golfer*. V.21, no. 1. January/February 2003. Midlothian, Virginia. 37.

4. Weymouth B. Crumpler. In a letter dated January 1996 to the James River Country Club. Published on the James River Country Club Web site, http://www. jrcc1932 .com/golfm.html. Accessed July 2003.

CHAPTER 7

"GIVE ME THE ANIMAL TO DO!"

1934–1936

ROCAS WAS THE ANTITHESIS of the cozy beach house Anna so loved at Brookgreen. But true to her nature of making the best of any situation and never looking back, and true also to the strong domestic streak in her makeup, she began the enormous task of creating a home out of the baronial Tudor manor house. Set in its 420 craggy acres of forest, traprock quarries and fields, Rocas was unlike any home Anna or Archer had lived in. An account by Anna's nephew, Brantz Mayor, gives us a hint at what the Huntingtons found after their return from Brookgreen in 1934.

"When Katz was wiped out by the stockmarket crash and departed with what he could pack in a suitcase, he left an elaborate house with twenty rooms wired for selected music, intercom, phones, etc. A livingroom that turned into an amphitheatre by the touch of a button with a full-sized movie screen. It had three theatre-size projectors ready for multi-feature showings. Between the house and some outbuildings was a half-sized olympic pool. The outbuildings included a large aviary cage plus a stable with riding horses.

"Uncle Archer filled the pool with topsoil for a garden and never used the selected musical installa-

tion which filled a room in the cellar. Aunt Anna filled the cages she found outside, and they both enjoyed the breathtaking view looking west across the Hudson. (The town of Haverstraw there today was then just a village of scattered houses, hardly visible below the cliffs where Rocas was.)

"One weekend there I was upset to see a lowboy dray, pulled by a tractor moving away from the main house loaded with possibly 2000 bottles in cases of every kind of hard liquor and wines. Uncle Archer had had a freight-handler clean out the walkin, temperature-controlled wine cellar. He wanted a few cases of his beloved Spanish wines and did not want to be confused by 'all that stuff.'"[1]

In her diary, Anna does not mention the kitchen or dining spaces at Rocas, important features of any Huntington residence because of how often they entertained at luncheons and high teas. Accordingly, we can assume the kitchen was well-equipped, that the linen closet, the pantry, and the china cupboards all measured up to Anna's exacting standards as a housekeeper.

Excited by the spaces outside, feeling healthy at last with fingers itching to dig into clay and mold it, Anna decided to do a series of wild animal sculptures.

Anna had cages built onto the kitchen wing of Rocas for a family of rhesus monkeys she bought from the Bronx Zoo to use as models. Then when Kelpie had her pups in 1937, the monkeys went back to the Zoo, and the cages were used for puppies and succeeding litters.

She had some paddocks, pens, and a monkey cage constructed near the kitchen wing and soon filled them with a small menagerie. From the Bronx Zoo whose director was a friend she got a family of three rhesus monkeys, a gregarious East Indian species with long brown hair. A pair of wild boars and bears with cubs were trapped in the nearby forest, and Archer helped her settle them in separate pens.

While the animals grew accustomed to their new "homes," she did studies of a pet greyhound, Echo, to test her fingers and see how it was to work with a wire tool again. She did *Echo Lying Down, Echo Licking, Echo with Old Shoe, Echo Startled.* These were small pieces, cast in aluminum and eight to ten inches high. Then gaining confidence, she tackled a larger piece, *Echo Scratching Behind Ear*, twenty-three inches high. Liking to work on several different subjects simultaneously, she alternated with molding birds she had observed in the Brookgreen marshes, swans,

an angry crane, a marabou, a fish hawk with a catch in its beak.[2]

Encouraged by how responsive and capable her fingers still were after such a long idle interlude, she began studying her wild menagerie. Archer helped her. One day when she was standing by a pen observing the boars, the female scrambled over the four-foot enclosure, mad with fright, and viciously attacked a horse grazing nearby. Fortunately, Archer had his pistol and shot the "poor wild thing." Her mate fought to climb out of the pen, snarling savagely and jumping up to hit Archer with his muddy snout. Later, the usually dignified bibliophile and poet, relished describing the "wounds" he sustained while protecting his own mate. (D1936, April 16, 24; May 10–15; July 4, 20)

Interacting with the monkeys triggered another incident. A prominent sculptor named Berthold Nebel who was doing a big job for Archer at the Hispanic Society, came to consult with Archer and brought his ten-year-old daughter, Lucia. While watching the monkeys swinging in their cage, one of them called Huey (after Huey Long) escaped, pounced on Lucia, and started to hug her. The child was terrified. Quick as a flash, Archer jumped to grab the scruffy brown imp by its neck and throw him back into the cage, slamming the door tight. Lucia never forgot the incident, remembering not only her fright but also how agile the huge Mr. Huntington showed himself to be.[3]

That summer Anna carved *Red Stags Fighting* and three studies of Huey, *Huey Cleaning his Coat, Reaching for Food*, and *Huey Climbing a Stick*. Later, she did a bronze *Wild Boar* standing guard over his mate asleep at his feet. During this creative explosion Anna produced some forty sculptures, all wild ani-

66

Diana of the Chase by Anna Vaughn Hyatt, 1922, in the reflecting pool at Brookgreen Gardens. The original *Diana* is in the rotunda of the National Academy of Design at 1083 Fifth Avenue, New York. Credit, Paul Hoffmann.

Jaguar Reaching, a bronze on limestone, 1906, at Brookgreen Gardens, by Anna Hyatt Huntington. Credit, Paul Hoffmann.

mals, in aluminum or bronze.[4] Bears, a vulture, and a jaguar were also included. Archer must have been pleased with the entire series, for in the summer of 1936 it was set up and exhibited on the brick terrace in front of the Hispanic Society.[5]

During that same year, Anna had a retrospective exhibit of 170 pieces at the American Academy of Arts and Letters. The recognition implicit in these exhibitions must have been heartwarming to Anna and Archer as well.[6]

Anna's predilection for sculpting animals has sometimes puzzled her admirers, especially when they see her exquisite *Diana of the Chase*, now in the center of a circular reflecting pool at Brookgreen

Gardens. "Find figure work very dull," she explained. "All figures are so alike that only the pose varies them. I do not see how sculptors can go on finding interest with only composition and design to vary. With animals it's different. You have tremendous variety and never the same in any way. Give me the animal to do!" (D1941, July 3)

* * *

To Anna's delight, in May 1935, a totally different kind of animal arrived at Rocas—a Scottish deerhound female puppy she named Kelpie. (D1935, April 16) She had decided to establish a kennel and Kelpie was to be the brood matron. Why, out of all the different breeds of dogs Anna chose this one, is a puzzle. In an essay found in her papers at Syracuse University, she cites the deerhound's gentle and friendly disposition. Its rich heritage was also appealing; the dogs dated from the ancient era of Scottish Highland Chieftans; it was found in tapestries and paintings as far back as the 16th century; Queen Victoria had a kennel of deerhounds at Balmoral; and Maida, a deerhound, was the favorite dog of Sir Walter Scott, Laird of Abbotsford.[7]

Another reason for choosing the Scottish deerhound could have been Anna's wish to promote the breed in this country, for its practical use in England and Scotland was fading due to quarries like deer diminishing with the industrialization of the land. Whatever the reasons, it was a fortunate choice. At a future residence in Connecticut, she and Archer were to derive immense pleasure and comfort from developing their kennel, having the dogs in their house and sharing their bedrooms, and from the affection of individual dogs, especially when Archer's

arthritis clouded his declining years and he was home almost all the time.

The deerhound is a big, rangy animal, three or more feet high at the shoulder, with a shaggy coat, blue-grey in color, that does not shed, and a docile nature. To be happy it needs space to move about and people to relate to. It would not be a good guard-dog; it is too friendly. During the summer at a dog show on Long Island, Anna learned there were only sixteen to thirty deerhounds in the United States. In September she found a deerhound club organized by the American Kennel Club. (D1936, September 15) Joining it, she found a breeder with a champion stud who lived in Orange County, Virginia, who would be glad to breed Kelpie when she was ready.

Anna probably hoped Archer would take to what would become a very large dog. But he was indifferent. This response or lack of it, did not disturb her for she recognized that for almost two years he had been uprooted from his customary patterns of interest and responsibility. Now, settling back into his familiar rhythm, he was being driven into New York City every week to visit the Hispanic Society. Before going abroad he had engaged several young and middle-aged women to take on some cataloguing and research assignments in the society's collections. Two had been sent to Spain to photograph and record daily life in the provinces of Galicia and Extremadura, where he had lived for two years in the 1890s. Still others were investigating microfilming and learning to use it as a practical way to make more books available.[8] So a priority on his agenda was finding out how his new recruits were doing and guiding their progress. One July day he invited eleven of them out to Rocas for luncheon, and Anna talked with and delighted in each one. She was so enthusiastic it seemed she had never met librarians before.

In addition to checking up on "his girls," on each trip into town, Archer would also visit the sculptor, Berthold Nebel, whom he had commissioned in 1929 to execute nine bas-relief panels for the society's outside wall on W 155th Street. Born in 1889 in Basel, Switzerland, Nebel had come to this country as a baby with his parents. As an adult he spent many hard years at the Art Student's League followed by a three-year fellowship from the American Academy in Rome. The experiences won him the post of Director of Sculpture at the Carnegie Institute of Technology, now Carnegie Mellon University, in Pittsburgh. Yearning to be in New York City, however, he gave up his directorship and settled in the Bible building on Astor Place in Greenwich Village. Then he set about getting commissions. Hearing about Nebel in 1928, Archer visited him in his studio. Following their conversation, the philanthropist suggested they take a ride in his limousine. "Bring a ruler," he said. The sculptor soon found himself at the Museum of the American Indian, one of the museums Archer had founded on Audubon Terrace. "See those old wooden doors?" asked Archer. "Make some bronze ones. Go ahead, anything you like."

Sometime later, with sketches approved, while Berthold was deep in casting the doors, Archer said casually, "Say, there are doors opposite at the American Geographical Society." Archer had founded this society also. "It wouldn't look right if they are not done too."

"Don't you want to wait until I've finished the first?" asked the sculptor.

"Michelangelo wouldn't have said that," said Archer.[9] Though Berthold protested he was no Michelangelo, he was thus started on a second major project. The bas-reliefs on the façade of the Hispanic Society Museum was Archer's third proposal. Each panel was to be five feet by eleven feet, mounted in a row, and should represent a people—Celt, Primitive Man, Roman, Carthaginian, Arab, Phoenician, Greek, Visigoth, and Christian Knight—who had, in turn, invaded and flourished in Spain.

In the fall of 1937 Archer made his regular visit to Nebel's studio. He said that his wife, Anna Hyatt Huntington, was working on a bas-relief of Don Quixote for the north wall of Audubon Terrace. In January she had completed the model for Rocinante, the Don's horse, and he, Archer, hoped Nebel would help her with enlarging the models as she progressed with them.

You see, in 1924, the sculptor had perfected and then patented an enlarging machine that enabled artists to make an exact reproduction of small models as one-quarter, half, or life-size. Ordinarily, this important step in a sculptor's work was done by what is called the point system—by measuring from point to point. But by comparison with using Nebel's device, this system of reproduction was clumsy and time-consuming. When word got out, sculptors pressed Nebel for work. Since he wanted time for his own creative work, the artist had to control the demand. However, in response to Archer's request, he would reserve time for Anna.

Archer was glad he could return to Rocas and tell Anna the contact she wanted had been made.

1. Brantz Mayor, "Uncle Archer." 7.

2. Edwards. 12.

3. Lucia Nebel White, inteviewed by Mary Mitchell and Albert Goodrich, October 11, 2001.

4. Edwards, 11.

5. *History of the Hispanic Society* 1954. Appendix VIII. 559.

6. Edwards, 11.

7. "Why I Chose the Deerhound." Undated manuscript, folder. Series III, Box 1. *AHH Papers*.

8. Proske. 11.

9. "Own Invention Robs Sculptor Nebel of Time." *Bridgeport Sunday Post*. n.d. 1957. 5.

CHAPTER 8

TRAVELS WITH DOGS, ARCHER, AND MOLDING OLD STEVIE

1937

ANNA'S "DOGGY YEAR," as she called it, began when the customized vehicle ordered three months ago arrived at Rocas. Designed to take them and their menagerie down to Brookgreen for the winter, it was outfitted with a Pullman-type bench for Archer to sleep on. Too tall, he could not recline.

For Anna, two questions loomed: How would the animals take the trip? And, more importantly, how would Archer like traveling with them? Typically, she never voiced a doubt and simply charged ahead as if nothing bothered her. With chauffeur McCarty at the wheel, they took off just before Christmas with four dogs including Kelpie, now six months old, three monkeys, and a macaw. Anna was aged 61 and Archer, 67.

The three-and-a-half-day journey took them through New Jersey and Delaware to the ferry at Cape Charles, Virginia, then through Norfolk to South Carolina.

"Echo (the greyhound) running up and down the aisle like a mad thing," she wrote, "was frightened by the noise of the engine and the heater. I was constantly on the move, feeding animals, cleaning cages,

keeping fire in the stove. Had a hot lunch and a thermos. Stopped frequently to let dogs out for exercise. Last time, 7:30 p.m., up every 2 hours to tend the fire as night was cold, car got frigid immediately. When fire went out monkeys would suffer. Heated up our lunch on alcohol burner. We are frozen by time to get dressed and hot drink very welcome, washing facility big as your hand. Kelpie good as gold, never fusses, just opposite of Echo. Up again every 2 hours to keep monkeys warm. Car dirty, impossible to clean." (D1936, December 21)

Arriving at Atalaya on Christmas Eve, the servants whom Anna engaged every year greeted them. The dogs raced about. The monkeys did gymnastics on the swings in their cage at the northwest corner of the house. The macaw went to her perch in the sunroom. Palmettos rustled in the courtyard and the sun poured in. Archer inspected the gardens, the new Negro village he had had constructed, and the 3000-gallon water tank in the Moorish water-tower. Observing that everyone, animals and Archer, seemed happy, Anna turned to a project she had had in mind since 1923. This was starting the bas-relief *Don*

Quixote for the courtyard at the Hispanic Society.

For some odd reason she found this difficult and had postponed it. In her diaries she does not mention reading *Don Quixote*, but her statue's design reveals she had, indeed, studied the novel. She knew which significant moment in his life she wanted to portray, and had a precise mental image of how the finished work should look. All Anna's equestrian statues, *Sybil Ludington, El Cid, Boabdil, General Israel Putnam*, reveal this perceptive approach. Each one, however, was a historical figure who had lived, died, and was a hero or a martyr. The Don, on the other hand, grew out of Cervantes' imagination. It had become a struggle to give shape to a literary figure.

Anna realized she must start with the figure she knew best—a horse. Rocinante, the Don's mount, must look as any horse ridden by an impractical visionary would look at the end of a crazy odyssey. Harriet Hyatt Mayor, a widow and Anna's sister, had come down to join the Huntingtons for the holidays. Seven years older than Anna, she lived in Princeton, N.J., in a house Archer had bought for her. Devoted to Harriet, Anna welcomed her company as moral support for her present initiative. "Now," said Anna, as they drove past some fields full of weeds, "keep your eye peeled for a bony old nag." Suddenly, Harriet pointed to a muddy farmyard. "Just what I wanted," cried Anna, "an old hopeless stallion, starved and wretched." (D1937, January 5) She found the farmer, paid him $25 and hired him to walk the horse back to Atalaya.

After five days en route, Old Stevie arrived. To beef up his strength, Anna fed him a special mixture of ground oats, middlings, cornmeal, and cottonseed meal. So weak he could scarcely stand up, she had a sling wrapped around his abdomen to steady him. Then, since it was important for her concept to have the model show how emaciated Rocinante was, she had his rough, fur-like coat clipped so the hollows in front of his hips would be revealed. Old Stevie gave her two weeks as a model. Then, fatter and feeling his oats, he bared his teeth, jumped and kicked in his stall. No longer useful, her first model finished, she had him put out to graze. (D1937, January 10, 16, 18, 20; February 8, 17) Such was the beginning of one of Anna's most brilliant and popular sculptures.

Five years later, in 1942, the statue of Rocinante and his Don, carved in relief, was finished and mounted on the courtyard wall opposite the Hispanic Society building in New York City.[1] It was a triumph of willpower and dedication for Anna. It shows the Don as he sets out on his mission.[2] Wearing mediaeval armor, this aged dreamer roamed La Mancha, his home-province, as a knight-errant in the Age of Chivalry. Throughout his wanderings he interpreted the mundane as opportunity for adventure. He mistook inns for castles, windmills for giants, flocks of sheep for opposing armies. On return to his village home, his helmet gone, his lance broken, defeated by reality, he sits in his saddle still erect and looking ahead, the feckless idealist who has forgotten the necessities of life such as feeding his faithful steed. The poor starved animal has to nibble on weeds in the road to find nourishment.

That winter, relieved and happy to have *Don Quixote* underway at last, Anna began additional projects she had laid aside while working on Rocinante. She took out of storage sculptures that had arrived in the previous fall and consulted with Archer, supervising their placement in the gardens. Frank Tarbox,

The customized trailer Archer bought to take the deer-hounds down to Brookgreen as well as to shows on Long Island, southern New York State, and elsewhere. It had a Pullman-shaped bench for Archer to rest on.

the landscape architect Archer had engaged to direct the gardens' development, participated in every decision. When the weather cooperated with a series of clear, sunny days and temperatures in the 50s, she started riding again, on her horses, Polly and Bob. Using color film, she photographed rosy sunsets. She even tried her hand at surf-fishing, but finding the undertow too heavy, had to stop, a big disappointment. She felt so well that she refused all invitations to lunch or to speak. Time at Atalaya was too short.

Kelpie came in heat, and arrangements were made to breed her to the stud Anna had located in Virginia. Randall, who worked for Archer, drove her to the kennel where Kelpie mated twice with the imported Scottish champion, Chad of Enterkind. Apparently, it took. The vet predicted she would whelp in late June. (D1937, April 21)

Archer, however, was growing discontented and restless. Anna noticed this in March when she tried

her hand at modeling a fountain-figure. He told her to stop—this was the architect's job, she should not interfere. (D1937, March 2) So seldom did he intrude on what she was doing, she said nothing and abandoned her design.

One day in March he told Anna he had just had the fiftieth interruption in his work. Fed up with the constant personal demands from everyone who came near him, especially those of the Negroes, he had told the men he was stopping the farm. All horses and mules were to go to Randall's place at North Creek. The cows and the bull must be sold. Telling Randall, his foreman, to dismiss a Negro named Willie, Randall blew up. "If Willie goes," he cried, "I go too." So Archer replied quietly, "Mr. Randall, I accept your resignation." (D1937, May 23) Shocked, Randall did go. Seeing Archer so irascible, Anna suggested motoring to Florida. To her surprise, Archer agreed. Before they left, he grumbled they might not return next year: "We might spend time on the other side where I can find peace to write and get away from nagging people, if they do not start another war before then." (D1937, March 3)

In April and May they made two week-long trips in their car with its trailer. The first took them to Winter Haven, Florida, where they put up in a trailer camp. For exercise and a view of the landscape, they climbed "a tower all cream and pink, very theatrical and sentimental, just what our moronic public eats up." (D1937, March 14) In Sarasota they saw the Ringling Museum and watched the winter circus exercises. From Palm Beach they drove to St. Augustine, enjoying the tree-ripened fruit. Always sleeping in the trailer, refusing invitations from friends to stay in their guestrooms, they did not enter a single hotel.

Anna's reward came when she heard Archer say: "This is the way to travel. Most enjoyable." (D1937, March 21)

Another trip they made was to Lexington, Kentucky, to see Man O' War, the renowned stallion and winner of twenty out of twenty-one races in 1919 and 1920. Although racehorses never attracted Anna's artistic eye, she wanted to see what one of the most famous of his kind was like. "He's a wonder, so much personality." (D1937, May 12) The Huntingtons continued on a kind of sentimental journey through Huntington, West Virginia, where as a young man Henry Edwards Huntington, Archer's cousin, had operated a sawmill for his uncle, Collis P. Huntington. (Collis and Henry's father, Solon Huntington, the oldest of the clan, were brothers.) Rising early at 5:30, they drove through the Appalachian mountains along the Kanawha River. Archer remembered climbing as a boy with his father when Collis was building the Chesapeake & Ohio Railroad in the region. It was becoming typical that in White Sulphur Springs where they could have stayed at the luxurious Greenbrier Hotel, Anna and Archer preferred to spend the night parked behind a gas station. Then through Roanoke, Virginia, Winston-Salem, and the Shenandoah Valley, back to Brookgreen. (D1937, May 31)

On return, Archer was in a more positive mood and began planning with a new foreman where ditches should be dug to improve the irrigation system for the gardens. He then started legal proceedings with his New York lawyer to make Atalaya entirely separate from Brookgreen. This made Anna wonder if, indeed, they would return the next year. It was her habit never to plan ahead, just let the calendar unfold and then cope with whatever came along. So she didn't query Archer about their future.

Back at Rocas in June, the animals settled into their old habits. The vet came to file the horses' teeth, and the dogs ate up the hoof-parings. Henrique, the head-monkey, sat on Anna's shoulder and affectionately nibbled at her ear. Archer drove into the city for meetings at the Hispanic Society. Anna, the parameters of whose life would soon be determined by a strange new challenge, called a carpenter to prepare a box big enough for a deerhound bitch, who would whelp anywhere from five to thirteen puppies.

When it was finished the box was put in their bedroom. On June 24, as Kelpie began to tear up newspapers in her bed, Anna and Archer hauled chaise lounges into the room. This was Anna's suggestion, and when Archer didn't demur, she was secretly delighted and relieved. They would share the vigil together.

---

1. *History of the Hispanic Society of America.* Appendix VIII. 559.

2. Edwards, 65.

CHAPTER 9

"DAFFY OVER DEERHOUNDS"

1937–1938

IT IS HARD TO IMAGINE Archer Huntington in a kennel-helper's role, but that is precisely what he became in the next few weeks. On the night of June 24 Kelpie's contractions began. An intense emotional experience followed for Anna and Archer, neither one of whom had ever had children. Anna was now to see a side of her austere and fastidious husband, a tenderness, that further endeared him to her.

"It was fortunate the vet was there," she wrote, "as receiving the puppies was a strenuous job, the tearing off of the envelope must be done instantly and the afterbirth caught as he doesn't believe in the bitch eating this. He dips the pups in very hot water, what your hand can bear, to stimulate them; then dries them in a rough towel. He received 7 pups, 3 dead, and started to leave because he thought she would want to rest. But he had hardly gone when more pups came and trotted along every 20 minutes until there had come eleven, only six living, and two looked puny. Kelpie did not have much pain only a few whimpers, the pups very small. It's a relief to have it over. We did not get to bed until 11:30 p.m."

The next four days passed without letup. "Up at 5:30 to feed pups as I had to have them for the night in my dressingroom. Shall have to devote all my time

to them . . . All day with puppies, giving Kelpie milk and eggs, all she will eat. She frets if she has to leave them. Have to remove them at night as she steps on them. Glad we did not invite anyone out this Sunday. Archer is worn out as he insists on helping during the night. The vet visits every day, giving Kelpie calcium in her vein. He seems a good intelligent vet, a Canadian which accounts for his intelligence.

"July thunderstorm so heavy Archer got up around 10 p.m. and went out to comfort Kelpie and take hot milk to the pups; the cook and maid offered to stay with her. All the household devoted to dogs. To celebrate, we went into the city and lunched at the Waldorf Roof, then went to the Radio City ballet." (D1937, June 24–28; July 1)

Anna was discovering that puppies and sculpture do not mix. For the time-being she laid her modeling tools to rest. As it turned out, they rested for five years more as she unexpectedly found herself becoming "daffy over deerhounds." (D1948, April 29)

* * *

WHEN ANNA started building up her kennel, she wrote only four entries about it in her diary. This is puzzling for she usually recorded new initiatives for

75

later reference. The first was the account of Kelpie whelping in June 1937. The second happened on October 14 when she registered four pups, the strongest and best, with the American Kennel Club, stating their place of birth as "Stanerigg Kennel." (D1937, October 14) (Stanerigg is the Scottish name for "stony ridge" and is pronounced Stan-rig as in dig. It later became the name of the Huntingtons' estate in Redding, Connecticut.) The third entry was four words long: "7 imported dogs arrived." This shipment, which arrived in August of '38, included the famous English Deerhound Champion, Prophetic of Ross, born in 1931, and acquired from his breeders, the Misses M. F. and H. M. Laughrey of Londonderry, England. Always treated as a house pet, they had sold him with Anna's promise he would never live in a kennel. At Rocas he became known as "Garth" and slept in the Huntingtons' bedroom. Does Anna tell about this champion who became the bulwark stud of her Kennel? No. Not a word.

Still another note tells how two of Garth's pups by a Stanerigg bitch named Dinsome tumbled down off a 25-foot ledge. The first got up and scrambled off, and the second sustained a broken foot. This suggests that Anna had as yet not delegated anyone to watch the youngsters.

Nothing more about kennel activity is mentioned until time to get ready for the annual trip to Brookgreen departing in December 1938. Even then, all Anna wrote was that they were taking 16 pups and 12 adults with them in a customized bus. We only find out that a sizeable kennel had been built near Atalaya the year before by seeing a photograph of it in an article published October 1939, in the *American Kennel Gazette*. The illustrations show several of the dogs

Anna feeding her dogs snacks after the daily hike of two or three miles around Lake Hopewell at Stanerigg. The estate had some eight miles of interlocking trails and graveled roads for exercising the deerhounds.

resting on the sandy beach after chasing seagulls up and down the oceanfront.[1]

If it weren't for the *Gazette* article and another from *Town and Country*, we would learn nothing about what was involved with raising Scottish deerhounds. The reporter for the *Gazette*, Arthur Frederick Jones, a true dog lover, writes at length about it. "Deerhounds need a lot of personal attention," he writes. "To keep them in top condition, a rigorous daily schedule of feeding and exercise is followed." Describing the kennel's routine, he says that adults get one or two miles a day running along rough country trails to keep feet and muscles hard. As for meals, in the morning each gets two eggs and milk. In late afternoon, comes the main meal. This consists of approximately two lbs of chopped beef, vegetable, a little suet and garlic, and dry dog food.

Archer with Chloe, whom he bought in a pet shop in Montreux, Switzerland. Credit, Brantz Mayor.

With eye of sloe, / And ear not low, / With horse's breast, / And deep in chest, / And broad in loin, / And strong in groin, / And nape set far behind the head— / These were dogs that Fingal bred. –An old rhyme. Found in Box 3, Series 4, Anna Hyatt Huntington Papers, Syracuse University Library.

Housing at Rocas, he says, is ideal. It is outdoors in heated houses set in a little colony built near the crest of the mountain. Often the adult dogs are let out to have the freedom of the entire place, the estate being secured by a heavy, high chain-link fence. The pups occupy cages that used to house monkeys.

"Mrs. Huntington takes a deep personal interest in her kennel," writes Mr. Jones, "and is never hap-pier than when caring for her dogs. Men on the place do the heavy work, but the owner and Miss Jean Smith, her Scottish studio assistant, supervise everything, care for the puppies, walk the dogs and handle the feeding. Invariably, she looks at an animal to study lines and proportions. As a sculptor she is well acquainted with anatomy, which is the foundation for all judging. So it is not surprising that she started off with Prophetic of Ross, who has the best blood-lines available. He has won no less than 12 challenge certificates, equivalent to four championships, in Irish and English shows. When Mrs. Huntington showed me her kennel, the big dog was beside her all the time. Apparently, he concluded that I was harmless and loved dogs, for after we returned to her studio in the house, Garth extended his paw and rested his muzzle on my knee."[2]

Wondering why Anna wrote so little about building up her kennel, one must speculate. There is no doubt she was busy and at night, tired out. She may also have been embarrassed by all the trouble she was causing Archer, who had to put up with the upheaval caused by integrating 28 vigorous big animals into their design for living. If left to himself, he would have chosen a toy poodle or bulldog.

And so again, there arises the question: why did Anna choose the breed of Scottish Deerhound. Memos written at the end of her diaries for 1938 and 1939 give one answer. "This has been a break away from studio work. It has been good for me. As when only in the studio I did not get enough out of doors. This year has been very hard manual work but mostly out of doors. It has greatly strengthened me physically." (D1939, MEMO, December 3) Anna had learned from her bouts with TB how important regular outdoor exercise was in keeping up her health. She wanted dogs that would force her to exercise daily outdoors.

Then, as one reviews Anna's life as a whole, another reason comes to mind. Before marrying Archer, she had to support herself as a professional artist and took great pride in being able to do so. Once married, she did not have to earn a living. Even

though she had hundreds of sculptures to her credit, she never sold a single one after marriage. She gave all away. When Archer gave her generous annuities to support her various endeavors, he had told her that she "could run the farm on my own income and attend to everything that did not have to do with construction and upkeep. He would take care of that." (D1940 June 4, 11) Operating Stanerigg Kennel satisfied Anna's physical needs as well as her consuming desire to show Archer and herself that she could run a successful commercial venture.

Still another answer seems likely. Having never had children, Anna had deep reservoirs of affection to lavish on living beings worthy of her attention. She developed enormous respect for her deerhounds. As her "doggy" story unfolds, we shall see how she loved her dogs with her whole heart and cared for them as if they were her children.

* * *

AS FOR ARCHER, while the commotion caused by kennel activity escalated, he tolerated it, but held himself aloof from participation, although occasionally if a dog was in the hospital quarters, he would tell Anna she must not cross over the road after dark to take care of the dog. He would take the night shift. Travel offered a welcome, manifest escape. In May of '38 he and Anna took a cruise on the S.S. *Bremen* and drove through Switzerland and France. This was immediately followed by another cruise on the S.S. *Queen Mary* to visit Mediterranean ports. On his passport for 1933 Archer had listed his profession as "Capitalist." In 1938 he called himself "Author."[3] The change of identity was justified since he had published several books of poetry in the interim.[4]

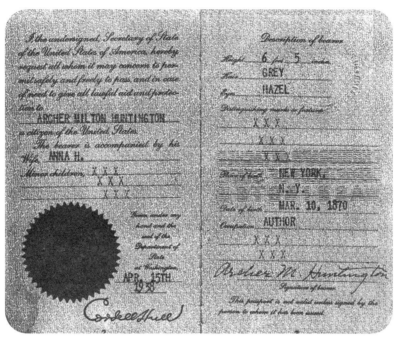

Archer's passport for 1938 used for two cruises, the first in May 1938, on the SS *Bremen* to Northern Europe; the second, in June 1938, on the SS *Queen Mary*, to the Mediterranean Sea. Anna never had her own passport. Courtesy, Anna Hyatt Huntington Papers. Syracuse University Library. Special Collections.

Edging toward retirement, he now saw himself as more of a literary man than as a philanthropist, though he never ceased being the latter.

Once back at Rocas, with the dogs content in a routine supervised by a professional dog-handler whom Anna had hired, a peaceful summer stretched ahead, with no hint at the upheaval and turmoil the late summer would bring. Archer enjoyed traveling to New York to the Hispanic Society to review and guide the work of the six women curators he had engaged in the departments of Bibliography, Ceramics, Costume, Pottery, Textiles, and Sculpture. All were researching articles on Hispanic topics, and he was proud of their work.

Keeping track of another project to do with maps also interested him. The World's Fair was scheduled to open in Summer 1939. For an exhibition at the Portuguese pavilion a curator at the American Geographic Society, which Archer had founded, was preparing a six-foot photographic facsimile of the Vespucci World Map of 1539. The cartographer was Juan Vespucci, nephew of the famous Amerigo Vespucci, Italian navigator, after whom this continent was named. The young Vespucci had charted the coasts of Central and South America as far south as Brazil, declaring this was the "New World," not Asia.

Then, without warning, the idyllic summer came to an end. In late August, as Archer sat in the garden at Rocas sunning himself, he noticed a small airplane circling low over head. It descended so close he could hear the pilot shout to his passengers, "Look! Look down there. That's where the Huntingtons live!"

Archer marched into the house to find Anna. "We cannot live here," he declared. "There is no peace. We must move."[5]

Thus an act of God occurred that would change the course of their lives forever.

1. "Stanerigg's Aid Renews Scottish Deerhound Favor in the United States." Arthur Frederick Jones. *American Kennel Gazette.* October 1939; 1941–2. 18–21; 16–19. Series IV, Box 5. *Published Material.* AHH Papers.

2. Ibid. October 1939. 21.

3. Passport, 1930. #158311. Folder Series II, Box 9. AHH Papers. Passport, 1938, #515244. See same folder and box. Individual photographs of Anna and of Archer appear on the passports. Both documents are in Archer's name. Anna does not have her own passport.

4. Books of poetry by AMH published by the Hispanic Society of America. Appendix VII. 555. *Rimas* 1936; *A Flight of Birds* 1938; *Spain and Africa* 1943; *Recuerdos* 1949; *Versos* 1952; *The Torch Bearers* 1954. (*The Torch Bearers* was published privately.)

5. G-M, *El Poeta.* 483f.

CHAPTER 10

"A CHIP OFF THAT SPLENDID OLD BLOCK!"

1939–1940

· PART ONE ·

ONCE HE HAD MADE a decision and cleared it with Anna, Archer didn't let grass grow under his feet. They decided to investigate an estate of some 500 acres in western Connecticut that was advertised in a magazine called *Country Life In America*. The advertisement showed an enticing view of Hopewell Lake, the largest of a chain of five on the estate. On October 18, when the foliage was at its peak, Anna and Archer drove to Bethel to the house of Howard R. Briscoe, the agent handling the property. Mostly in Redding, some of it spilled over into Bethel and Newtown.

Mr. Briscoe, to whom they had telephoned ahead, was expecting them. Later, he told a reporter, "I saw an enormous limousine with liveried chauffeur pull up in front of my house and out stepped a huge and handsome man holding a copy of a magazine, Mrs. Huntington was with him. They asked to see the property advertised. I suggested that their car be parked at my house, and I would drive them around in my less conspicuous Ford."[1]

While driving through the rugged Connecticut landscape, past hogbacks, stony ledges, and thickets of evergreen and laurel, Briscoe recounted the history of the estate. Set on the high ground between Sunset Hill Road in Redding and the Newtown Turnpike, its rocky reaches were known in Indian times as Wiantenuck, a name used today by the Weantinogue Land Trust. Some early settlers named Couch moved in to clear and farm the land.

Then followed three wealthy owners. First came Vermont Senator Peck whose wife was a Wells of Wells Fargo. The second was Walther Lüttgen, German partner in the international banking house of August Belmont. Lüttgen was a member of nine clubs in New York, including two yachting clubs. By 1909 he and his wife had built and were living in "Villa Linta" on Sunset Hill Road. Something of an engineer, he erected dams to create five lagoons all connected together. Then he would entertain guests by cruising them around the lagoons while he was at the helm of a small paddlewheel steamer, wearing a commodore's cap. The story goes that he intentionally sank the steamer when a friend pointed out he could be ruined if the boat sank or burned with a load of guests. Another story said he sank his nautical toy when the town levied personal property taxes on it. Whatever its fate, no trace of it has as yet been found in the lagoons.

The Commodore did not stop with the view from the lakes. Wanting his guests to appreciate his spacious properties, he built a network of wide, graded carriage drives from one end to the other. Originally surfaced with gravel, today, the roads are still there, uncommonly beautiful as they wind past rocky outcrops and evergreen clumps on one side and on the other, crystal-clear lagoons.

At age 83 this colorful figure died. A year later Joseph E. Sterrett, once president of Price, Waterhouse & Co., and his wife bought the estate. An avid gardener, Mrs. Sterrett created an elaborate garden shaped like an oval in front of the villa. Little is known of the Sterretts. He died in 1934. Sometime in the late 1930s, a spectacular fire destroyed the villa and its gardens (but not its well-fertilized soil so useful to Anna when she would develop her Victory gardens here during World War II). Widow Sterrett lived with her Great Dane for a short time after the fire in a cottage near the intersection of Old Dodgingtown Road and Sunset Hill Road. Then she asked Mr. Briscoe to put the place on the market. This accounts for the arrival of Mr. and Mrs. Archer M. Huntington.

The asking price for the estate was $150,000. Once he found what he wanted, Archer never dragged his feet. So without any discussion, he told Briscoe that his lawyer at Cadwallader, Wickersham & Taft on Wall Street in New York would prepare a deed. Everything went off without a hitch. Anna and Archer soon became the owner of 552.41 acres of the Nutmeg State.[2] Like Mark Twain who came in 1909

and never left it, the Huntingtons chose Redding to be their home for the rest of their days.

After leaving Briscoe, Anna and Archer wanted to lunch at an Inn called The Spinning Wheel. "It was too crowded so lunched at a roadside place. It had a machine," wrote Anna. "You drop 5 cents and it plays." (D1938, October 18) Surfeited by the dose of history Briscoe had dealt them, all she could record in her diary was the novelty of finding a juke-box to play in a roadside café.

At the same time Archer pondered why living in this part of rocky Connecticut so appealed to him. One reason was its remoteness from New York and the difficulty money-seekers would have trying to locate him. More important, though, was being in a region where his father had grown up. At age fifteen in a town called Harwinton west of Hartford, Collis was apprenticed to a neighbor named Phineas Noble who had a small store in the front room of his house.

"Young Collis bedazzled Mr. Noble by memorizing both the wholesale and retail cost of every item in the cluttered stock," writes David Lavender in his biography of Collis, "and then calculating without pen or paper or even moving his lips the profit that could be expected from each piece, either in cash or barter. Won over by such virtuosity, Noble loaded a wagon with slow-moving items and sent the overgrown boy peddling them door-to-door through the countryside.[3] It was 1849. Collis soon left Noble to join up with Solon, his older brother, and take the Panama route to Sacramento, California. Here they set up a store in a tent for the rowdy goldminers whose pockets bulged with cash. From then on, Collis's story was hard work, success, and wealth.

Driving through the towns of Torrington, Litchfield and Woodbury, remembering the tales his father had told him about his youth, Archer felt he was on a sentimental journey. Here, in the wild, rustic countryside, were his father's roots. He liked to recall how Collis had brought him up as his own son. Perhaps he had peddled notions on the very roads they were driving on. This was a stirring thought.

Anna also felt an affinity with rocky New England, having spent summers as a child on a farm in northeastern Massachusetts. In December, after their trip through Connecticut, she had written, "I wish we lived on a little farm with just 2 people to take care of us, a few cows, chickens and dogs and never had to go anywhere, either winter or summer." (D1937, December 2) Anna yearned for a farm. She was to get it and a studio, too, but not quite in the modest dimension she imagined. Driving over the eight miles of hilly roads on the estate, she also knew that here was the ideal setting for Scottish Deerhounds to grow up in and thrive, and for her to walk them every day.

Returning from Connecticut they started preparations for their usual winter holiday in Brookgreen. Before leaving Archer had a heartwarming surprise that came out of a clear blue sky. Cuba conferred on him the title of Commander or Liberator. (D1939, November 8) So when D-Day for Brookgreen arrived, he was in a spirited mood. Hyatt Mayor and his wife, Virginia, came to celebrate. "After a lunch of caviar, pheasant, and chocolate icecream, he kept us all in a gale of laughter. He got all his affairs attended to so had a peaceful departure instead of the usual hectic one." (D1939, December 20)

This year, though, now that Archer had deeded Atalaya over to Brookgreen and the Huntingtons were anticipating the move to Connecticut, living there had a different feel. The place was not theirs anymore. Anna felt as though she was marking time until they could return to Rocas and she could think about starting a studio again after the move. An exhibit of twenty-five pieces representative of her forty years as a sculptor, plus some new studies of wild birds from Brookgreen, was traveling around the country and winning praise. "I am getting itchy fingers to sculpt again. Perhaps I am 'some pumkin'. The old lady had better do some 'pretty things' before she totters into her grave." (D1939, February 15)

Soon after returning in April, as spring unfolded, they went to Bethel to plan their coming move, meet the architect, and decide where the house and the kennel should be placed. This time Archer did not design the house himself. He engaged an architect named Atterbury who was disappointed "that we wanted such an unarchitectural structure for a house and the kennels so large and long. In fact, he seemed rather hostile, hating this kind of job." (D1939, June 20)

A conventional designer, Mr. Atterbury was taken aback to hear what his clients wanted. The house was to be "two-story, with a flat roof, and made of cinder blocks. Doors between the rooms must be steel; beams for the flat roof sheathed in copper, and the floor covered with a polished concrete mix. The entire structure must be fireproof. As for the kennel, it should have a large kitchen with counter for preparing the dogs' meals, and an apartment above for Jean, the Scottish kennel-keeper. It is to be finished by Christmas 1939 when we must move the dogs into it." (D1939, June 20)

Archer then told the architect to prepare blueprints for house and kennel. The ugly sand oval where Villa Linta had stood was beside the central road. They chose a setting for "Stanerigg," as the place was to be called, south of the oval. The house was to run east and west, with the front door facing north and have a south exposure for the living room. The studio was to be at the eastern end with a north exposure and a full two stories high. The kennel was to be across the road and a big garage built on the space left by Villa Linta. They found an ideal fellow named Ferry who had a small farm nearby, to be their farmer. Realizing weather might be colder in Connecticut, on her next trip into New York, Anna fetched Mother Huntington's sable coat 40 years old, out of storage, for use "up north." (D1939, September 26)

Anna's memo for 1939 reveals her long-term plans. "Putting most of the dogs under a kennel man will give me time to get back into a studio and perhaps finish the Hispanic Society work that Archer is so anxious for me to do." (D1939, MEMO, December 31) This meant finishing *Don Quixote* and creating the bas-relief *Boabdil* for the courtyard's wall. Archer might be anticipating retirement, but the word was not in Anna's vocabulary. She looked ahead to renewing her sculptural career as soon as they moved.

"This has been a radical year for Archer deciding to build a new house and change to new quarters. But it seems even if we have one foot in the grave a sensible thing to do for our declining few years.

"The place (Rocas) has to be kept up with 5 men just to make it look respectable; whereas the same number of men on a farm will give us fruit, vegetables, eggs. Here as quite simple-living people we are in a false position. We dislike display and want only what is needed for the simple comforts of our age.

"I hope Archer will get more uninterrupted work on the farm as it's too far away for frequent trips to town or many visitors to come out; also the place is too small for any large luncheon of 20. 6 will be our limit. The staff will be smaller, too." (D1939, MEMO, December 31)

Evidently, harmony began to reign between architect and clients, for the Huntingtons had him choose the paint color for the interior of the house, and invited Mr. and Mrs. Atterbury for lunch. The kennel was finished by New Year, and twenty deerhounds and pups settled into the new quarters. K. J. Hedengren and his wife, both Swedish, who were experienced doghandlers, took over the two-story apartment and began caring for the dogs. (Jean Smith was still in the Stanerigg picture, helping Anna with the dogs. But it is not clear where she lived.)

At Rocas Anna and Archer prepared to move. And on September 16, 1940, after "mountains of trunks" were loaded into a van, the long-awaited transfer was made.

(Although Redding was where the Huntingtons voted and paid taxes, Bethel was where they had their post office box. Much closer by road than Redding to Stanerigg, Bethel was where they shopped for groceries, kept a freezer container, and was the address on their stationery. Bethel was also where the depot for the New York train was located.)

· PART TWO ·

TWO IMPORTANT EVENTS occurred in 1939 and 1940 that concerned Archer, not Anna, although she benefited indirectly from the second one. In October

Members of the American Academy of Arts and Letters in the *Members' Room with Academy Chairs, December 6, 1923.* Seated (l to r) Robert Underwood Johnson, Owen Wister, Bliss Perry, Joseph Pennell, Archer M. Huntington. Standing (l to r) Nicholas Murray Butler, Charles Dana Gibson, John Charles Van Dyke, Arthur Twining Hadley, Hamlin Garland, Augustus Thomas, Daniel Chester French. The Academy buildings in classic Beaux Arts design, opposite each other on Audubon Terrace, were built in 1923 and 1930. Financed by Archer Huntington, they have been placed on the National Register of Historic Places in New York City Landmarks. Courtesy, Collection, American Academy of Arts and Letters.

of 1939, "an intramural battle known in its day as 'the Row'" erupted between the National Institute of Arts and Letters and the American Academy of Arts and Letters.[4] When this happened, Archer found himself in the thick of things. The Institute's elections of such advanced writers as Carl Sandburg and Sinclair Lewis, Ezra Pound and John Steinbeck, and others, had begun to disturb the older, more conservative members of the Academy, of which Archer was a director.

"They had come to feel that the Institute was a lost cause from which the Academy might do well to divorce itself," wrote Geoffrey T. Hellman. "Its president, Nicholas Murray Butler, who was backed by Archer Huntington, had special reason for favoring this move. For one thing, he wanted to get General John J. Pershing, then seventy-eight, into the Institute, as a stepping-stone to the Academy. It was hard to fit him into the Institute's Department of Literature, Department of Art, or Department of Music,

85

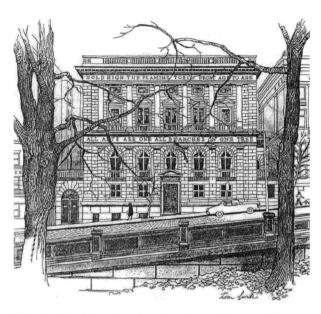

The façade of the American Academy of Arts and Letters built in 1923 at the southwest corner of Audubon Terrace. It faces onto West 155th Street. Credit, Tom Funk. *The New Yorker.* Copyright 1976. Reprinted by permission. All rights reserved.

but if the Academy were to set itself up independently, with the power to choose members whether or not they belonged to the Institute, might not Pershing be admitted to the shrine?"[5]

Archer tried to resolve the dispute by introducing a resolution that would free the Academy by the simple process of striking from its constitution the sentence: "Only members of the National Institute of Arts and Letters shall be eligible for election to the Academy."[6] This was carried with only one negative vote, and other members of the Academy were informed by mail of the proposed amendment. One of them was Walter Damrosch, who was also president of the Institute. He was outraged by the idea of the upper-house child's leaving its lower-house parent, and mounted an energetic opposition which motivated representative members of the Institute to call on Dr. Butler in his office at Columbia University.

Immediately taking charge of the discussion, "Dr. Butler said the whole thing arose out of Mr. Huntington's insistence that greater dignity should be given to the Academy by its having the right to elect such members as it chose . . . He (Dr. Butler) had labored with Mr. Huntington, giving the impression that Mr. Huntington was very obstinate and had it so much at heart that if the amendment were not passed, he would resign from the Academy, would give no more contributions to the Academy and would alter the provisions of his will."[7]

Not only had Archer given land at Audubon Terrace to the two institutions, but he and his mother had donated $200,000 to build permanent homes for both of them, the Institute in 1921, and then the Academy, in 1929. In 1917, Charitable Gift Deduction was voted into the tax code. Archer and Arabella may have been taking advantage of this, for between 1921 and 1930, Archer gave both institutions around two million dollars in checks, securities and real estate . . . Both were occupied by 1930. (This gift included the $660,000 Archer received from Sir Joseph Duveen for Rembrandt's painting, *Aristotle Contemplating the Bust of Homer*.)

"The battle was soon resumed in all its polite fury," continued Mr. Hellman. "Walter Damrosch led the opposition to the amendment that Archer was supporting, canvassing his fellow-Academicians by letter and telegram, asking them to express their opposition to the amendment, and most of them complied. In the middle of May the Institute's disloyal daughter, the Academy, gave up. At a meeting of the Academy's board, Huntington presented a resolution that was unanimously carried. "The directors, acting for the Academy, for the time being, waive the right to elect members outside the Institute . . . Later, Huntington and Butler resigned from office, and the Academy's great angel said that he would never pass its portals again. He never did, nor did Butler. The Huntington benefactions ceased."[8] (The story of "the Row" is now ancient history. Read No. 9 in the Notes to this chapter to find out about the American Academy of Arts and Letters today.[9])

They did cease except for a mystifying fifty thousand dollars, "perhaps tax motivated" wrote Hellman. More than likely the gift was Archer's gesture of gratitude to an institution that had admitted him for his scholarship, not for his money. Archer's wealth may have been inherited and he never had to work for his living as had many of the Institute's members. He was self-taught. His erudition was due not to any formal academic education in a university, but to his own determination to learn and the power of his native intellectual drive and genius.

* * *

THE SECOND RED-LETTER EVENT to do with Archer took place six months later in May 1940. By this time he had purchased the Connecticut estate in Redding and was taking steps to shed responsibilities, as one by one, at irregular times, the opportunity arose and he could do so. On May 10 one of the most onerous came to a head, namely, ownership of the Newport News Shipbuilding and Drydock Company based in Norfolk, Virginia, called the Yard.

Archer's association with the Yard went back to 1890 when he visited the shipyard with his father who founded it in 1886. While Collis was busy in meetings he amused himself by watching construction. He did not know the drydocks were strictly guarded, and that entry was forbidden without a pass. Approaching one of the docks he met a big Norwegian guard who asked him for his pass. While explaining who he was, the guard gave him a heavy blow, knocking him down. Humiliated, Archer stood up, shook the dust from his clothes, and when back in New York, joined an Athletic Club. Here he had William Muldoon, trainer of the prize fighter, John L. Sullivan, give him boxing lessons.

The next time he visited the Yard, he went out to the docks. The same brutish Norwegian was still there, as yet unaware of whom he was confronting.

"You have a pass, eh?" he said.

"No, it isn't necessary," answered Archer.

"Now, I teach you a lesson," growled the guard.

As he advanced Archer struck him with a hook to the jaw, raised him up in the air, and then saw him collapse on the ground, knocked out. Somebody nearby splashed a pail of water on the guard's face to arouse him, and then when he came to, told him who his opponent was. The guard faltered, afraid of losing his job. Wanting to reassure him, Acher shook his hand and said, "Don't worry. Now we are even."[10]

At that time, hoping his son would carry on his business interests, Collis had Archer work at the Yard and study navigation. Archer did learn business management and got an insight into sound business principles. But when Collis proposed making him manager of the shipyards, Archer refused the offer. He said he wanted to become a scholar and builder of museums. His father let him do as he wished, only asking him to do it well. Collis did not like mediocrity, and he raised his son with that philosophy.[11]

Over the years Archer followed his father's credo, did become a fine scholar, and built some fifteen or more museums. His favorite, and perhaps the one as successful as Brookgreen, was the Mariners' Museum and wildlife refuge near the Yard. On 1000 acres of beautifuly landscaped grounds a large dam was constructed to create Lake Maury of 145 acres. Migrating wild fowl and other inland animals like turkeys, deer, and swan, found sanctuary in the lake's many inlets and ponds. Archer said this was the second in a chain of wild life refuges, Brookgreen being the first.

In this setting, in 1931, while building Atalaya at Brookgreen, Archer had the museum and a library built. "In its charter, the museum proposes to build, own, equip, maintain and operate a museum and library pertaining to nautical subjects, things and interests, and otherwise to advance learning, the arts, and sciences related to or bearing on water crafts, the marine and marine navigation, thus to promote the public welfare . . . and incident to the whole, to develop and maintain a lake and park within the bounds of which the foregoing purposes may be accomplished."

As usual Archer dictated how the museum should be built. It is a one-story, fireproof structure of concrete, granite, and brick laid up in a peculiar way called "The Huntington Squeeze," the same as was used in building Atalaya. The mason lays a brick in place, spreads mortar lavishly on top, and then places the next brick on top of the first, squeezing it down so that the mortar oozes out. He doesn't scrape it away but leaves it to dry. The result is a rough wall-

Conquering the Wild by Anna Hyatt Huntington 1934, at the Lake Maury Park of the Mariners' Museum. The statue is dedicated to Collis Potter Huntington 1821–1900, founder of the shipyard. Credit, A. S. Goodrich.

surface with an attractive textured look when the sun glances across it.

Inside the Mariners' Museum, the displays have an enormous diversity. Collections of small vessels from all over the world stand next to a cluster of ocean-buoys, some well over 15′ in height. Glass cases hold scrimshaw and postage stamps with marine subjects. Engineers traveled all over the world gathering objects and making copies of what Archer and Homer Ferguson, retired director of the

The original bronze doors to the Mariners' Museum, by Herbert Adams. The museum built in 1931 and 1932 was constructed of brick laid up in the "Huntington Squeeze" pattern. The Moorish design appealed to Archer, and Atalaya, the Mariners' Museum, and Stanerigg were all built this way. The Museum is now the library. Courtesy, Mariners' Museum Archives.

Yard, wanted, so that staffs of researchers could plan exhibits to display everything, once the cases were constructed.[12] When the museum outgrew itself, a much more spacious display-wing was added, and the library, also growing, moved into the original museum building.

* * *

WHEN THE TIME CAME to sell the Yard, the museum and the wildlife refuge remained separate and independent. Here, a little background is neces-sary to understand what Archer accomplished. In 1900 when Collis died, he left the Yard to Arabella, his wife. During her lifetime, Henry E. Huntington, her second husband and Archer's cousin, tried to per-suade her to sell the Yard. But she put her foot down. She said Collis had built it, left it to her, and she did not want to sell. Then, at her death in 1924, Henry Huntington inherited it. In 1927 Henry died, and Archer, as head of the family, became president, owning three-quarters of the 100,000 shares of stock.[13] With the book value of the plant and property as of April 27, 1940, amounting to $17,792,644, the company was "probably the best known shipyard in the United States."[14] From time to time Archer had turned down offers to buy it. Finally, in May of 1940, he announced it was for sale.

On May 7 Archer and Anna stayed in town to meet with the three parties who submitted the highest bids. "One named Fell was so sure he could win," recorded Anna, "that he submitted a $500,000 certified check as down payment before the bids were opened. Other bids ran from 160 per share to 165, which was Archer's guess. Then he opened another for 176 with a covering letter of 4 points more making it 180. This took Archer's breath away. After much talk Archer won every point and ended up making them do what their bank said was impossible." (D1940, May 7) The buyer, a syndicate of underwriters, paid around $18 million for the stock.[15] Charles W. Butterworth, Archer's lawyer, said later that two of the bidders had "a sort of remembrance about Archer. They acknowledged he had completely dominated them all and called him 'a real chip off the splendid old block.'" (D1940, May 7)

1. Frank W. Nye. "The History of Huntington Park." n.d.

2. Sterret to AMH. 18 January 1939. AMH Papers.

3. David Lavender. *The Great Persuader: The Biography of Collis P. Huntington*. University Press of Colorado, Nimot, Colorado. 1969. 2f.

4. Geoffrey T. Hellman. "Some Splendid and Admirable People." Profile. *The New Yorker*. 23 February 1976. 72.

5. Ibid., 71.

6. Ibid., 73.

7. Ibid., 73.

8. Ibid., 74.

9. Ibid., 74. The story of "the Row" and Archer Huntington's part in it is now ancient history. "In 1976, after 72 years of separate though related existence, the National Institute of Arts and Letters and the American Academy of Arts and Letters voted for a merger that made them one institution with a single Board of Directors, committee structure, and budget, retaining, however, two levels of membership. From 1976 to 1993, the institution was known as the American Academy and Institute of Arts and Letters." This move was called *The Merger* . . . In *The Present*: "In 1992, the members of the Academy and the Institute voted to dissolve the Institute and unite into a single body of 250 members, which began 1993 as the American Academy of Arts and Letters." The history of *The Merger* and the report on *The Present* are quoted verbatim from *Publication 421*, revised 1996, which was kindly given to us by the American Academy of Arts and Letters in June 2003.

10. G-M, *El Poeta*. 27.

11. Proske. 2.

12. "The World's Largest Ship Museum." *Baltimore Sun*. 11 December 1932. No page number.

13. Thorpe. *Henry Edwards Huntington*. 368.

14. William L. Tazewell. *Newport News Shipbuilding: The First Century*. 1938. 155.

15. Ibid., 155.

CHAPTER 11

"A YEAR TO LOOK BACK ON"

1941

THE HOUSE THAT ARCHER BUILT stretched along a high ridge on Sunset Hill Road in Redding. On New Year's Day it was sunny, no wind, and temperatures ranged between 29 and 41. Anna, in a worn old sweater and work-boots, a key-chain dangling from her belt with keys in her pocket, stepped out of the studio to survey the scene. "All the men off and away. Will have plenty to do with Jean (kennel-maid) and Ferry off too. Will have dogs and horses to do. Archer is having a grand undisturbed day, altering his will and adding codicils." (D1941, January 1) Just before moving to Stanerigg, Archer had given Anna three generous annuities, saying he wanted to be sure she was taken care of. He also told her that she could run the farm with income from the annuities, and that he would take care of construction and upkeep. (D1940, June 8, 11) Pleased that he trusted her judgment about spending money, Anna looked forward eagerly to developing the farm. She had dreamed of having a farm for a long time.

Three months earlier, the Huntingtons had moved from Rocas with sixty rooms into Stanerigg with twenty rooms. Inside, there was no waste space. Outside, the exterior of the new house made of cinder blocks looked austere and uninviting. One per-

son called it "a monstrosity," another, a "penitentiary," and still another, "a concrete block monastery." The Huntingtons couldn't have cared less. Inside, they were comfortable, safe and cozy, and in hot weather the house would be cool.

A frequent visitor was Anna's friend and assistant, Lucia Nebel, who was 22 years old and the daughter of Berthold Nebel, the Swiss sculptor described earlier. Lucia had turned out to be an able photographer, and came whenever Anna wanted a piece of work photographed at a certain stage in its creation. The Nebels lived in Westport, a town only half an hour by car away.

In her late seventies today, Lucia remembers what Stanerigg was like.[1] She recalls a big red couch fitted into a wide, square bay window that protruded out from the big living room and faced south. Stanerigg was 1,000 feet above sea-level, and from the roof on a clear day, Lucia could see Long Island Sound. She also remembers that the walls were hung with etchings by Sir Edwin Landseer, a Victorian landscape painter who loved deerhounds and English hunting scenes, particularly a scene when the hounds had a stag cornered in a rocky outcropping on the moor. For Christmas Anna liked giving friends a calendar

The front façade of Stanerigg, the Huntingtons' residence in Redding, Connecticut, on Sunset Hill Road. Built in 1940, over the fifteen years of Archer's time there, and until Anna died in 1973, it became a mecca for all kinds of people, family, scholars, artists, Spanish immigrants, indigent professors and clerics. Anna ran a household that kept Archer supremely happy . . . An outsize set of blueprints which A. S. Goodrich studied at Syracuse, showed him how to label the rooms with their special functions. Once Anna died and the estate became the Collis P. Huntington State Park, the house was demolished and the property was purchased for a riding stable and school.

with a photograph of a Landseer etching for each month. Lucia photographed the etchings, one by one, for Anna to use in her next calendar. No sculpture was displayed in the house anywhere.

To the left of the front entrance down a long hall was Anna's office, and opposite was Archer's book-lined study. Beside his big desk was a small one for Miss Perkins, his secretary. Next to the office was his library-space where he had been arranging books on shelves, books brought from Rocas and No. 1 East Eighty-ninth Street in New York, to Stanerigg in a

large van, four trunks, fourteen boxes, and forty-eight cases in total. "It's a wonder where he'll find room for them," wrote Anna. As time passed, he didn't. The overflow had to be stacked in the back hall between his and Anna's offices. Near his office was the elevator, and across the hall, a dining room to seat only six or eight people, designed small because the Huntingtons wanted to limit themselves to only a few friends at a time.[2]

At the east end of the house was Anna's big studio, two stories high, with a floor-to-ceiling skylight fac-

The kennels under construction in 1940. They accommodated up to thirty dogs, had a large kitchen for preparing deer-hound meals, a hospital and a well-lighted place for grooming. After Anna's death, the kennels were made into apartments.

ing north, bare whitewashed walls and a long medieval tapestry that was once Arabella's, covering the south wall. The unheated studio had its own fire-place and heater, and an entrance from the driveway big enough to admit an automobile.[3]

Outside, north of the Big House, was the foundation where the Villa Linta had once stood. Here now was a big new garage, and beyond that the long kennel made of cinderblocks with twenty fenced-in runs for the deerhounds. With the cow barn near the big garden, cow manure, compost, and water handy, by August the big garden was producing enough to keep Anna in a non-stop bustle of picking, preserving, and packing for the freezer. By early fall the place was a productive, working farm.

While feeding the Huntington household, the farm also produced enough vegetables and eggs necessary to keep deerhounds in tiptop condition, whether for sale or for show. Ferry, the farmer, had already constructed a chicken coop for 175 White Minorcan hens and was building up the dairy herd to have cows for milk etc. and beef cattle to slaughter as

necessary for the household and the dogs. In Winsted, a town north of Redding, he had bought six well-bred Guernsey cows and a pedigreed Guernsey bull named Dol-King. The bull was a big, powerful fellow who had his own stonewalled pen at the end of the farm-road. Ferry also arranged with a veterinarian who promised to bring Dol-King's semen to a cow when she freshened and try three times for a fee of $5. Anna was proud of having her dairy be useful to the kennel as well as the household.

With wartime restrictions on buying farm machinery now being enforced, she was unable to find a combine to cut and thresh oats, so Ferry was told to clear precious pastureland and plant it with corn and grains. At Sears Roebuck in Danbury Anna found a tractor, a cultivator and extra freezer for vegetable and berry crops. During August and September the housekeeper, Annie McKinnon, came up from No. 1 East Eighty-ninth Street in New York to stay and help Anna cook and package produce for the freezer. On the day the root cellar was finished, she stored fifteen jars of tomatoes, jelly made from three pails of crabapples, and twenty-eight jars of cranberry jam. Remembering how her mother used to show off her cellar shelves with their rows of vegetables and fruits in Mason jars, she took Archer down to look at her husbandry. He was impressed, but when she told him the tractor cost $8170 "he did not like my spending that much for farm machinery. But if I had spent it on clothes he would not have protested. On the other hand I would have been ashamed to spend it on clothes." (D1949, February 1)

After laying out the garden, Babon, a hired hand, told her he was amazed at how many rocks he and his crew had dug out everywhere. Before long Anna had him constructing a rock wall to enclose a compost bed. Workmen came to plant young crabapple trees around the driveway, and start grapevines climbing over a stone wall. Propelled by boundless energy, Anna was out all day, orchestrating the operations. "So nice to be working on the grounds. At Rocas. I couldn't. Too many gardeners around." (D1941, April 29)

A good part of the time at Stanerigg, Anna and Archer lived in separate worlds. Anna's world was outside in the farmyard, the kennel, and in her studio, but inside, Archer's kingdom was his big office. He worked on his poetry and writing and reviewed the work of the Hispanic Society curators who came to Stanerigg to see him every few weeks. He never interfered with Anna's farm operation. Nothing about it appealed to him.

The Huntingtons planned to visit Brookgreen in the spring, but before going Archer needed to see his lawyer. At 5 p.m., March 12, Butterworth met them in their New York home with a deed for Anna and Archer to sign to transfer Atalaya and its surround-

ing property over to Brookgreen Gardens. Wanting to deliver this important document personally to the Gardens, the Huntingtons left the next day by train via Richmond for Georgetown, South Carolina. From there, a car drove them to Brookgreen.

They stayed at Atalaya for three weeks. They delivered the deed, reviewed the Gardens and placement of sculpture with the horticulturist Frank G. Tarbox, and visited the zoo to see the otter in the pond and watch the swans. "The old cob attacked Hovey (the driver), caught hold of his pants and tried to beat him with his wings. Hovey just took him by the neck and back and heaved him over into the pond," Anna noted in her diary. "The spunky old devil reared up and was ready to attack again." (D1941, March 26)

Together, Anna and Archer sorted out furnishings, leaving just the bare necessities for a future visit, if there was one, and sent off eight barrels and boxes by freight to Bethel. After a social three weeks, having old friends for tea or lunch, they left Brookgreen for Florence, South Carolina, to catch the crowded northbound Miami train. "Both A and I felt a difference in the place; it's not ours now. It's just as beautiful, but it's done, and we are not essential to its wellbeing." (D1941, March 14)[4]

On return to Connecticut Anna was busy with spring planting, and Archer with appointments made before they went south. His first meeting was with Judge McMahon, whom he was consulting on taxes. For his Connecticut lawyer, Archer had picked one of the foremost attorneys in Fairfield County. He had met Judge McMahon when, as a witness, the judge signed the deed transferring Stanerigg to the Huntingtons. At the time, Leonard McMahon was

94

associate judge of the City Court, an appointment that did not prevent him from pursuing a private law practice. Nobody called him "Mr. McMahon." A highly respected, astute and agreeable fellow, he was always called "the Judge."[5] He came often to advise Archer; then he would shed his legal demeanor, bring his wife whom Anna found compatible, and his two bright children, and they would have a social visit.

In moving to western Connecticut away from the populous, wealthy east coast, Archer hoped to frustrate solicitors. But this was only a pipe-dream. No matter where he was, they ferreted him out. For instance, a Dr. Heil from California asked Archer's help with a Hearst monastery. Archer said he would not have anything to do with a Hearst project, adding that "it would be a fine thing for Frisco if an earthquake did not flatten it in time." (D1941, May 26) Church solicitors received similar snubs, brushed off with being told churches ought to economize, a rebuke Rev. Bull of the Episcopal church in Georgetown, S.C., was familiar with.

Others had better luck, and for good reason. Stephen Pell, director of the Museum at Fort Ticonderoga at the northern tip of Lake George, wanted support in restoring the bastions. They were crumbling. With his thorough accounting of costs involved in reconstructing the bastions, he caught Archer's interest. The elated young director left Stanerigg with a check for $33,000. (D1941, May 31)

A Dr. Filley and colleagues from the State Farm Bureau approached Archer about an experiment. He wanted to see how Siberian chestnut trees planted at Stanerigg would do in that setting. He described how this particular genus grew to massive propor-tions and how useful its timber was. Moreover, its nuts were edible. Europeans pulverized them to make flour for flavoring soups and cereals. Archer was so intrigued with the proposal that he fixed whiskey and sodas for his guests, and spent a jolly afternoon hobnobbing with them. (D1941, May 31) If Filley had just given him a sentimental pitch about preserving an endangered species, he would have left Stanerigg empty-handed. But as it was, he departed with a check for $10,000 and a plan to return. Anyone who solicited Archer with a sloppy contract, vague plans or specifications not supported by hard facts, would leave without a check and no return invitation.

Archer was hard-headed as a nut, but he did have a soft heart. The number of indigent old friends unable to get by in Florida on a meager income and middle-aged scholars who couldn't find a job, who visited him with their hands out and departed with a check or a promise of support, was legion, and his Yankee wife kept a wary eye on visitors with sob stories he might fall for.

Observing how intense was Archer's pleasure in his new workspace, Anna urged him to relax and do things with her outside. Glad to sense her concern, he helped her pick spinach, a long way down for someone 6′ 5″ tall. He even walked with her and four or five dogs around Hopewell Lake when his arthritis didn't hamper him. He also liked shopping at the A&P in Bethel, wheeling the market cart. This allowed him to peer over the tops of the cases and direct her which way to turn.

The new couple with an aristocratic air about them stirred up gossip. "Wherever we are," Anna wrote, "people stare at us with ardent curiosity as if there was something about us they could take home and talk about." (D1941, May 23) Far from being annoyed, Archer relished telling about the reputation he had gained with the townspeople. "The last time McCarty (the chauffeur) went to Bethel," he told luncheon guests, "he stopped to pick some lilies growing by the roadside. Soon a woman rushed out of a house across the road and grabbed them out of his hand. 'How dare you pluck those flowers! It's against the law,' she screamed. 'And who are you, anyway?' When he told her, she said, 'Well, you're as big a crook as your master.' She didn't know what to do with the lilies in her hand, so handed them back to him." (D1941, June 9)

* * *

ALTHOUGH BUSY with the farm, Anna was anxious to keep up her ties to the art world. Many small pieces of animal sculpture were stored in the basement at Stanerigg. So in the spring she wrote to museums across the country which had her bronzes, asking if they wanted another as a gift. From May through October there came a flood of enthusiastic responses; by the end of October she had donated sculptures to museums in 134 different cities. (D1941, May 1, 7, 15, 26; Sept. 18; Oct. 11, 26)

This affirmation of her current status in the sculptural community was encouraging, for she had at last begun to work on a subject that had been on her mind for fifteen years, a subject Archer was urging her to start and complete. This was the equestrian figure of Boabdil, intended for mounting as a bas-relief on the west courtyard wall behind the statue of El Cid at the Hispanic Society. The *Don Quixote* was

Boabdil, bronze plaque by Anna Hyatt Huntington. Bronze plaque at Brookgreen Gardens. Credit, A. S. Goodrich.

finished and at the stonecutter's, waiting to be mounted on the east wall back of El Cid.

Boabdil, or "the Arab," as Anna liked to call her subject, was the last Moorish sultan to rule in southern Spain after the Moors' seven centuries of occupation. The significant moment she chose was his abrupt departure from Granada after the Christian armies of Ferdinand and Isabella had defeated him.

The scene must have had tremendous drama. Here, at the foot of the snow-capped Sierra Nevada mountains, in a courtyard of the ancient turreted Alhambra, Boabdil surrendered the keys to Granada to the triumphant Spanish monarchs. Dressed in splendid robes, they were surrounded by knights and squires. Christopher Columbus who had just received the green light from their Majesties to finance his voyage to the Indies, was in the audience. "It was January 2, 1492," wrote Columbus in his diary. "I saw the flags of Our Majesties placed in the towers of the Alhambra. The Moorish King kissed their hands and departed from the gates of the city, followed by fifty faithful knights."[6]

As he left, a tearful Boabdil looked back over his right shoulder to gaze down one last time on his beloved pleasure gardens. In his *Tales of the Alhambra* Washington Irving tells how his mother taunted her son's tears with the cruel words, "You do well to weep like a woman for what you could not defend like a man."

Anna took a special amount of trouble in sculpting Boabdil. She found a model named Muchon who came to Stanerigg with his mother for ten days to pose sitting astride Anna's own riding horse named Prince. (Anna found accommodations for them in Bethel.) Prince was an old fat pet with nothing spirited about him. So Anna found an illustration of a bona fide Arab stallion to study for conformation. Feeling the saddle had to be genuine Arab too, she canvassed riding academies in Connecticut and New York State. After a month's search, one was found in New York City, and Miss Perkins was persuaded to bring out the awkward bundle to Stanerigg. (D1941, June 17; July 3, 8, 12; Dec. 4)

After moving into her studio Anna had had a scaffold built there with a chair she could sit or stand on. Now she climbed up onto the structure, carrying not only her tools but clay used in modeling the *Quixote*.

Then in July and August, between making crabapple jelly, freezing green beans, and canning tomatoes, she modeled the cloak onto the figure and the proper detail onto the saddle. For two years war and farm work interfered with finishing *Boabdil*. Archer was so pleased with the result he wrote a verse about it. (From a volume of poems entitled *Godoy*)

> *He wore a cloak of grandeur. It was bright*
> *With stolen promises and colours thin,*
> *But now and then the wind—the wind of night—*
> *Raised it and showed the broken thing within.*[7]

Meanwhile, throughout the year, the Huntingtons were acutely aware of the war raging between England and Germany. Anna bought Archer a bedside radio. He was at first so depressed by the news he didn't want to listen. Then as he heard Big Ben tolling in the background and Churchill's stirring oratory, he was hooked. Following General MacArthur's futile efforts to save the Philippines from the Japanese, kept him riveted. A confirmed Anglophile, Anna became actively involved. She and Jean, her kennel-keeper, collected fat from the house and the kennel to make soap for Bundles for Britain, and collected shoes, including her new unused riding boots, to ship with the soap. (D1941, December 17)

Anna and Archer heard about Pearl Harbor from Anna's nephew, Brantz Mayor, and his wife Evelyn, who lived in Mt. Kisco and came over for tea. (D1941, December 7) Afterwards, they kept the radio on for several days running. Meanwhile, Archer was excited to have a note from a lady in Haverstraw, New York, who asked if Rocas could be used for defense emergency as a temporary station for the wounded. Since he and Anna had left Rocas he had been unable to persuade two churches, the Christian Science church and the Roman Catholic church represented by Cardinal Spellman to take over the estate and maintain it until it could be sold. When the request came it seemed like manna from heaven, and he assured her Rocas was open for wartime use when needed. (D1941, December 19) As the alarming news panicked the nation, friends living far from New York City telegraphed the Huntingtons to join them in a safer place. Anna declined, writing, "Little old Connecticut is where we'll stick even if Hitler does come." (D1941, December 10)

The war news so distracted Archer that he locked his keys in his office. "I broke the glass like a burglar, climbed in the window, and got them," boasted Anna. "Not bad for 66!" (D1941, December 27)

A Memo closed her 1941 diary: "This has been a very busy and happy year up here on our hilltop. Luxuries like cars, refrigerators, washing machines etc., even stoves, are getting difficult to buy. Cars are off the market. At least we will have this year to look back on during the unpleasant times in store for us all." (D1941, MEMO, December 31)

1. Interview with Lucia Nebel White. 11 October 2001.

2. Blueprints of Stanerigg. Shelf List. Box 36. Oversized Package 6. General Files: House Blueprints. AHH Papers.

3. Ibid.

4. Atalaya is now maintained by the State of South Carolina which signed a fifty-year lease agreement in 1960 with Brookgreen Gardens for 2500 acres of oceanfront property to create a state park. Atalaya is on that property. Brookgreen is on the west side of U.S. Route 17, and Huntington Beach State Park is on the east. *Visitor's Guide to Huntington Beach State Park*. 1.

5. Leonard McMahon. *Obituary*. 6 September 1955. *Danbury News-Times*.

6. Ellen S. Hoffman. *Columbus' SPAIN*. Washington, D.C. 1992. 75–83.

7. The poem about Boabdil is by AMH and is inscribed under the bas-relief of Boabdil mounted on the wall of the Hispanic Society courtyard. *Boabdil* was mounted in November 1943. *HAS History*. Appendix VIII. 559.

CHAPTER 12

"WAR JITTERS"

1942–1945

· PART ONE: ANNA THE FARMER ·

IT WASN'T UNTIL EARLY 1942 that the war hit Anna personally. Robert Baillie, who had a stone-cutting workshop for sculptors in Closter, New Jersey, appeared at Stanerigg and asked Anna when the *Boabdil* model would be ready. His quarry was going to close; he had to know what to plan.

This news startled Anna. *Boabdil*, or "the Arab" as she called it, was the last equestrian figure to be finished to complete the *El Cid* ensemble for the Hispanic Society's courtyard. Preoccupied with buying livestock and directing her farmhands, she had been slow about modeling the Arab. Even Archer had visited her studio recently to ask how much longer she would be. Now the quarry was to close. She must finish the model.

Feeling under pressure, Anna managed to squeeze in an hour or two of work every day for the next two months, working on the horse's head, on the drapery of the Arab's cloak, on his harness . . . Gradually, piece by piece, she completed it. And in May, two of the work-crew carried the pieces to an empty corner in the kennel to await Contini's arrival. The stress caught up with Anna. On a short walk with Archer

around the cow barn and back, her pulse quickened, her heart pounded, and her sputum was bloody. Was this a TB flareup? She had to go to bed and rest.

Soon after, the kennel manager reported the harness on the Arab's neck had fallen off. Anna left her bed, went to the kennel, and repaired the model. (D1942, June 23) On the Fourth of July, Contini arrived to make the mold. He waited a few days until it hardened, then returned from his studio in New York to cart the big pieces away. Anna, who announced, "I shall never do another large piece of work" (D1942, July 8), sent the remaining plaster to the National Sculpture Society for members to use.

For two years, war and farm work interfered with getting *Boabdil* ready for mounting.

With the Arab gone, Anna's strength revived. The Office of Price Administration had clamped down on gas rationing, and the government was urging small farmers to make their farms as self-sufficient as possible. Building up the herd of cattle and developing her Victory garden became priorities for Anna. Dairy products and vegetables were necessary for her household and for feeding the deerhounds, which

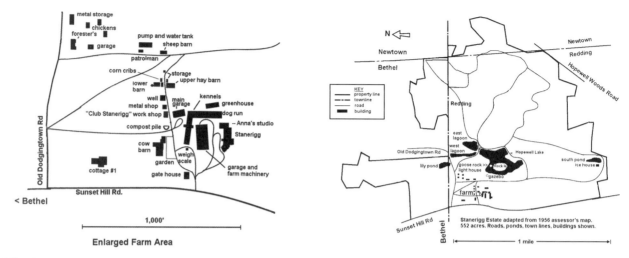

now numbered fifteen adults and an uncounted litter of pups. The State Farm Bureau had told her that an accredited (or in today's parlance, "certified") herd was a *must*. And it recommended Herefords for beef cattle. (D1942, November 2)

Anna relied upon Ferry, the strong intelligent fellow who had abandoned his own small farm and moved with his family into the Stanerigg gatehouse in October of 1940. Ferry had already prepared space for livestock. In the big old horse-barn formerly used by the Sterretts, he had removed the stalls and built in stanchions for dairy cows and had wired pens for their calves. Down the main road, he had remodeled the old haybarn to accommodate beef cattle. At the east end of the cart-road he built a large chicken coop for the Minorcans. Ferry also cleared brush and weeds and encroaching woods, and had fenced in lush green pastures of varying sizes

between the farm and the lake. The crew enjoyed it so much they didn't want to leave.

To acquire livestock, Ferry read classified ads in regional newspapers and kept his ears open. It was a time when many were quitting their farms and taking jobs in factories because they were unable to get hired help; their cattle were up for sale. By October of 1942, a small but well-bred herd of ten fawn-colored dairy cows munched hay contentedly, heads in their stanchions. The red-coated, white-faced Herefords occupied the former haybarn down the road near the corncrib, and every morning were driven out to pasture. The hens' eggs supplied the house as well as the kennel, two per day per dog, and excess was sold in Bethel and roundabout.

Stanerigg was quite a showpiece. With its red barns, small wooden sheds, the long Victory garden between kennel and cowbarn, all lined up along the central cart-road, the place looked like a farm-village.

In October Anna called the State Farm Bureau to report she now had a herd, and needed it inspected. When the inspector came, he tested all of the cattle for TB and brucellosis ("Bang's Disease," in collo-quial terms) and five days later, reported them clean. (D1942, October 30) If Anna breathed a sigh of relief, it was wasted. On April 3, one of the Hereford cows threw a premature calf. (D1943, April 3) With appre-hension Anna called the inspector to return. The calf had brucellosis and must be slaughtered.

If this infectious disease—a worry haunting every dairy farmer—was detected early enough, the calf would be aborted. Brucellosis affected humans, as well, and could cause the fatal undulant fever. So Ferry had the barn floors scrubbed and disinfected. Pigs that were likely carriers of the germ were moved to another barn. Anna waited, and hoped the spring air and fresh grassy pastures would work magic on the other cattle. It did. On June 7 of 1943, the dairy inspector, on his monthly round in western Con-necticut, reported that Stanerigg had a certified, grass-fed herd.

Anna may have rejoiced at finally having the farm of her dreams, but she had also discovered the expe-rience was not the bucolic idyll of her childhood. Wartime had altered everything. It meant filling out long questionnaires when applying for gas to run the tractor. She had to expect frequent and random vis-its from dairy inspectors. The county engineers also came unannounced to see why the barns used so much fuel. Anna had to queue up in a long line to submit to hard questioning by a stern ration board in Redding: Why did Stanerigg need so much fuel?

So many problems. The farm needed a silo, and the government ruled against building one now. Auto rental agencies had closed down, and Archer needed gas to get to New York to visit the Hispanic Society and his banks. Even in wartime, she had orders for deerhounds from as far away as Oregon, Minnesota, and Wisconsin. Uncooperative about shipping dogs, the railroads could not certify a safe arrival. At night, unable to sleep, Anna wondered how she would solve these issues.

Another headache was keeping domestic help. Anna learned never to put an Irish maid in the pantry with a Swede in the kitchen—to be more specific, the chambermaid and the downstairs waitress who lived on Stanerigg's second floor. One morning the two servants came down to breakfast reviling each other and announcing their immediate departure. One had her face scratched and the other's glasses had been torn off and crumpled. When Della, the Swedish cook, abruptly gave notice that she was leaving that day, Archer displayed a rare burst of anger. "Swedes are the limit," he said. "Never again. I'd like to pitch all damned Swedes off the place." Hedengren, the Swedish kennel manager who lived in the kennel apartment on the second floor and was an essential cog in Anna's wheel, was present to hear Archer's comments and clammed up. "He goes around like a thundercloud," wrote Anna. "I'd not exactly blame him." (D1941, July 14; D1944, July 17) A stoic Hedengren stayed three more years. And when he left, Jean moved into the kennel apartment.

The single compensating factor in the whole pic-ture was Ferry. He had gradually assembled a motley crew of five workmen, each too old or disabled to be drafted. Among them was Stanley, a Dane, whom

Anna set to work digging up and planting her Victory garden. In a memo written at the end of 1943, Anna describes the group of farmhands, a certain affection for these superannuated individuals emanating from her cryptic comments.

"None of them seem to agree or like each other. Each says the other is lazy and good for nothing or dishonest. Grindle, the Scotsman, a veteran of World War I, was gassed and has a wounded knee that still hurts. A good worker he has to be handled with gloves. But he does a lot. He keeps the garage and drives me down to Bethel to shop; he takes care of the poultry. He helps exercise the dogs. He thinks Congalles is a crook. (Congalles has the old stucco maintenance shop across from the main garage.) Congalles never complains or talks of other men to us. But his shop is their gathering place and of course, a place of gossip. I call it Stanerigg Club. Old Nicholson, 72, a New Englander, works hard and has to be held back from doing the other men's work. But he is the only one the others agree is a good one, and he in turn thinks all the others are good. They are not an easy group to handle, but we're fortunate to have them in wartime." (D1943, MEMO, December 31)

Anna knew she was lucky. The beef cattle were kept largely to provide meat for the men and their families, all of whom lived on the place in scattered cottages. Her studio had become a slaughterhouse. When a steer was slaughtered, Anna gave each man packaged meat, always hard to get and requiring the highest ration points. The Huntingtons often had turkeys and duck sent up from Brookgreen Gardens, sometimes 15 birds at a time. At Thanksgiving and Christmas, Anna gave a turkey to each family. And,

when Mrs. Grindle, for example, was sick and had to be hospitalized, Anna and Archer drove her to the hospital and then picked her up. They never hesitated to use anything in short supply, even tightly rationed gas, for the benefit of their employees.

During the war Bethel operated a large community freezer. Anna rented two big lockers, one for her household and the other for the men where they could keep their packaged meat. (Later, in 1944, when Anna decided to downsize the cattle herd to concentrate on milk and butter production, she had the Herefords slaughtered, one by one. Each Stanerigg Club member got his share.) They might not get along with each other, but each knew he had a good job with a caring boss and mistress in a difficult time, and each showed his appreciation by working hard at his own particular job.

In the summer of 1942 the garden was in full production. Like the previous summer, she cooked and packaged produce until the freezer was full to the brim. In Anna's day this achievement was like the cellar shelves that Mother Hyatt had showed off every fall in Annisquam; it testified to her husbandry.

Despite the demands wartime imposed at Stanerigg, Anna found the energy to help others in need. For months before Pearl Harbor, when the British were at war, she had knit socks, gathered wool scraps and used clothing for Bundles for Britain. Eager to continue helping, Anna worked with her kennel manager to gather up fat from the kennel, studio, and Big House kitchen, and render it into soap. One time Anna gave Bundles fifty-eight cakes of homemade soap, another time, forty-eight. The smell of fat being rendered pervaded the entire house; Archer would try to escape it by closing his office door.

After Pearl Harbor, Red Cross units soon sprang up all across the country and Danbury became a focus for units in western Connecticut. Anna immediately wanted to pitch in and start a Red Cross unit at the farm. "Sunset Hill where Stanerigg is has a small community that is rather isolated these gasless days," said Anna to freelance writer Jane Dillon, who wrote an article on Anna and Stanerigg for the *Christian Science Monitor* in September 1943. "None of us felt we could take the time or spare the tires to go four or five miles to the nearest Red Cross unit for war work. So the Danbury Red Cross Chapter kindly allowed us to set up our own unit." (D1943, July 25; September 11)

Anna didn't tell Miss Dillon the trouble she ran into at the outset, but wrote about it in her diary. "Seems my starting a RC unit is causing hatred and heartburn in Redding Ridge. They spread petty lies about me. One woman said that at war bonds meeting I insisted on showing my deerhounds and tried to get her to buy one. This is a deliberate lie. She was a vixen type of French woman, her husband a former Hitler. I am extremely glad our place is no nearer to Redding Ridge as there seem to be trivial, unpleasant people there." (D1943, June 13) When Anna had first approached Miss Sanford, head of the Redding unit, she received a brisk "NO!" No consultation. (D1943, March 7) Opposition to the idea was so fierce, one woman declared the Stanerigg unit would start over her dead body. (D1943, June 22)

At the end of March, however, a visit from the head of the Danbury Chapter (accompanied by a chastened Miss Sanford) rewarded Anna's forbearance. She was told to collect twelve women to meet every week on Thursday afternoons, to come to Danbury for instructions on how to fold and make the bandages, and get materials from Redding and return the made dressings there. (D1943, March 23) On June 10, wrote Anna, "We had a great ruckus as 17 women showed up, green but eager to learn what to do. The bandage-machine worked well, especially with the smaller bandages. The workers enjoyed themselves." (D1943, June 10)

At first all bandages had to be inspected and many redone. "It's astonishing," commented Anna, "how unskillful some women are with their hands." (D1943, August 30) Helping Anna was Mrs. Helen Lalley, a pleasant able young woman whose husband was away at bootcamp, and who had applied to Anna for the position of bookkeeper. Mrs. Lalley made herself so essential that if she was absent, Anna would postpone the meeting. For the next eighteen months, until mid-July 1944, between nine and fifteen women met regularly in an unoccupied, but furnished cottage with a furnace and running water on Sunset Hill Road on Stanerigg property.

The unit's anniversary of June 8, 1944, coincided with D-Day news and the successful invasion of Normandy by the Allied armies. Anna celebrated both events with coffee, sandwiches and cake, and presented each worker with a ceremonial button and striped ribbon. A great occasion, everyone talked at once. (D1944, June 8) And Anna's biggest reward came when several told her how pleasant it had been to work at Stanerigg rather than in the usual school storeroom setting. The unit continued to meet, as regularly as flu-epidemics, the canning season, and blizzards allowed, until July when Mrs. Lalley had to leave for a while to help a sick sister in Philadelphia. When the group tapered off, Anna did not push to keep it going, nor did the Danbury Chapter urge her to. It was August. She had to get ready to cook and preserve, and fill the freezer. She, herself, was tired.

The past few months had been difficult. At the end of March, "the snake struck again. Examination shows sputum positive and I am in bed to stay. Poor Archer—it's a bad blow to have to see me through a second TB fight." (D1944, March 30)

In those days, the doctor made house visits and even brought along a machine to X-ray the chest. It took three visits with his machine before he could tell Anna her bronchial tubes were normal size. On May 6 she listened to the Kentucky Derby on the radio from her bed. On May 13 she went downstairs for the first time for lunch. Fruit-trees were blooming, and a rose tree flowered for the first time.

Confined to her bedroom for six weeks, Anna breathed sighs of relief when the maids said they would all stay. "They said I was the kindest mistress they had ever served. This really made me feel good." (D1944, April 3) The members of Stanerigg Club took on extra work without grumbling. Grindle agreed to drive the little car to exercise the dogs and found it so enjoyable he continued after Anna was well. Once downstairs and back to normal, Anna and Archer decided, regardless of gas rationing, to celebrate her good health by having a "High Tea," the kind of Sunday affair she remembered her parents used to give on the farm at Annisquam. This meant a mix of many friends who had carte blanche to bring their own friends as well. How they all managed with the stringent gas rationing, is a wonder. There was "an etcher with a broad accent who looked very foreign like Hungarian or Slav and a husband full of stories and adventure. They have houses in London,

Tangiers, and Marrakesh. Stuart Grumman was a Princeton classmate who spoke excellent Spanish." (D1944, August 13) Anna served tea from a simple wooden table with drop leaves; Archer cut generous slices of cake made with the last of their hoarded sugar while Garth, the household deerhound, hovered nearby to get his deserved share.

The next day Anna walked around the lake with a few dogs, the first time since March, happy to be well again.

It is obvious from the entries in her diaries for 1944 and 1945 that Anna's bout with TB was a turning-point. She must curtail the scope of the farm-operation. She could not chance another bout with "the snake." Other things changed, also. Anna abandoned exercising her deerhounds by driving a horse-driven carriage with the dogs tied behind—the strain on her arms was too strong. (D1944, November 29) And when she turned to the easier task of driving what was called the "dog-car," Archer put his foot down. "No," he said. And then told Grindle he must take over the job. It was the first time in many years Archer had interfered with Anna's activities; she was taken aback. (D1943, October 10)

When another Hereford tested positive for brucellosis, and had to be trucked to Hartford to be slaughtered, Anna decided to get rid of the Herefords. "Bad investment, these beef cattle." (D1943, December 22; December 29) Butcher Schenik from Bridgeport started the operation, which Anna felt compelled to watch. The Herefords with their bull strength and thick, red, wavy coats had an ancient, godlike quality. Observing their demise was to Anna, the artist, like watching Götterdämmerung.

"Went down to see the work. Very skillfully done.

For their daily outings dogs were tethered to the MG, and precious gas was used to exercise them. At first in 1945 Anna drove the car. She had just recovered from a TB flareup. Archer stepped in and said: "NO. Grimble will do it after this." This was one of the three or four times in their marriage that Archer told Anna she could not do something.

Joints severed with ease and skin taken quickly. It was a bloody sight but one some artist should have painted as it took place in a corner of the hay barn. With the carcass hanging on high, blood over the floor and yellow and purple intestines spread out, the carcass yellow against the dark interior and the men in blue jeans working with gleaming knives, it was a true Rembrandt lighting and setting." (D1944, February 9)

The kennel, at first so sacred an ingredient in Anna's plan for Stanerigg, was the next "victim." Clearly the frustrations of wartime rationing contributed to the decision to downsize. Supplies of horsemeat were irregular, and Archer had helped Anna buy a ten-foot freezer to hoard meat against periodic shortages. But twice they needed to spend precious gas to drive to Bloomfield, north of Hartford, to pick up the meat. That was the last straw.

First to go was the large dog trailer used to carry several dogs at a time to shows. ("I'm burning all my bridges to any showing of many Deerhounds.") (D1944, May 17) Then Anna decided to remodel the entire west end of the kennel. Part became an overflow coop for pullets, who settled into their fancy new quarters and began laying fifty to sixty eggs daily. Another section was boarded off for pigs. Ten were sold; and when another had a litter of eleven, Anna declared, "No more sows or pigs." (D1945, November 7) Space was cleared for Ferry and his hired help to kill and dress the remaining ten hogs, 300 pounds each. This produced useful space. Into it went files, typewriter, and furniture brought over from the Big House so that Anna could settle in there and keep the kennel books.

How many dogs remained is unclear. Thirteen had been sold in 1942. No bitches were bred. About ten hounds, perhaps, still had to be walked, brushed, and given the affectionate care Anna loved to provide. Sales had continued, and even during the war, requests to buy deerhounds still had come from as far away as the Midwest.

The loss of Garth had been a severe blow. In July of 1944 when he turned twelve, he had started a downhill slide, growing inert and showing no appetite. On September 12 Anna wrote, "Poor old Garth eating less and less and reduced to a skeleton. Every move is an effort." Finally, on October 3 "we made up our minds to have Garth put to sleep and called Strassburger to do it. He went peacefully but it took a large dose to put him out." (D1944, October 3)

Anna was heartbroken. Their house pet for six years, Garth had sired three wonderful litters and given Stanerigg the cachet his English breeders had predicted he would do. He had followed Anna everywhere. When she had a letter to mail, he had learned to get up from the floor at her feet and lick the stamp. Since 1938, after arriving at Rocas, he had been a bulwark and their bedroom companion. Was his death a premonition? Only time would tell if Stanerigg Kennel would survive.

· PART TWO: ARCHER RETIRED ·

YOU MAY HAVE NOTICED how seldom Archer's name appears in this chapter. His wartime world differed from Anna's—it was inside and sedentary, unless, that is, he was in New York. Physically and mentally, he was in a frustrating, painful period, worse than ever before. By early 1944, his arthritic hips and legs were so crippling that he was embarrassed to walk across a public dining room to lunch with a friend. He could no longer take regular walks with Anna, around the farm, or go shopping with her in Bethel. His need of her helping arm, her concern, her companionship, was acute and increasing. Sensitive to this, Anna was glad she could now leave the farm to Ferry and accompany Archer to New York whenever he needed her, which was every time he went.

Gas rationing had eliminated the car rental service he had counted on for years, and the train was now the common transport for business travelers. His height and bulk made it hard to stretch out his limbs in the seat, and leg-cramps compounded the discomfort. Needing to go to the City for business reasons, he appealed to his New York physician who gave him a letter confirming his need for a car and driver to make the round trip between Bethel and New York. The ration board granted clearance.

His New York City world was vital to him. Born and bred a New Yorker his activities there had always been central to his life. No. 1 East Eighty-ninth Street was the Huntingtons' home-away-from-home, and they had been accustomed to coming into the City once or twice a month to stay a few days. It was a convenient place to entertain and meet with his lawyer, banking officers, or a physician. Brookgreen board meetings were always held in the middle of May when Anna would have Sherry's or Longchamps cater gourmet luncheons. Typically, on entering the house, Anna would call, "Archer, are you there?" Then she would hear a disembodied, muffled voice from far above. "I'm up here, in the library."

Archer had other New York "homes." These were in the vaults of the Guaranty Trust, the Central Hanover Bank, and the Bank of New York. He kept his bonds, securities, land deeds and deeds of trust, his most important papers, in these banks. Two or three times a year he would take Anna, and go down into a cubicle, lit by a single bulb, shut the door tightly, and open the long tin box crammed with documents. Reluctant to trust everything to just one bank, he had divided them among three banks, some 120 bonds with coupons to cut, Anna cutting and Archer listing, each coupon. (D1949, February 24) The job would take an entire morning. "Good to have it done with." (D1949, March 15)

Another home was the Hispanic Society where he never failed to stop or visit the staff, and where he had his own office near the entrance from the brick terrace off Broadway. On the wall opposite his big desk hung the seven-foot portrait of himself by José López Mezquita. He was devoted to the place as president and founder and kept close track of what the young women curators were doing. He always wanted to prove to the museum community that women could work as librarians and administrators as well as men could.

Besides being president of the Hispanic Society, he was chief officer of the Brookgreen Gardens, an effective force in the National Academy of Design and in the American Numismatic Society. "In the range of his talents, the strength of his enthusiasm, and how he has chosen to use his wealth and power," wrote John K. Wright in the *History of the American Geographic Society*, "there is something in Mr. Huntington that suggests a humanist prince of the Renaissance. Tall, dignified, massive of build, he dom-inates without being domineering over whatever group he may join. Friendly, democratic, and buoyant, his mind and imagination work at high speed, often enigmatically. He is at times, a bit baffling, especially when with tongue in cheek, he comes forth with a truly outrageous question or comment to see how it will be taken. He knows men in and out, and sees through pose, pretence, and insincerity with a probing eye."[1]

In 1944, though, there was one occasion when this masterful prince of the Arts found himself unwittingly backed into a corner. Often the people he dealt with were temperamental, talented artists who needed special treatment. At Brookgreen in September of '44, for example, he had to settle a dispute between Robert Baillie, the curator of sculpture, and Adolf A. Weinman, a sculptor. At this time Baillie was so upset, he took the train in wartime up to Bethel to visit Stanerigg and tell Archer what he had done.

Archer had commissioned Weinman, a gifted artist, to do a large limestone statue for the gardens called *Riders of the Dawn*.[2] It was to be a major composition to anchor a space adjoining the display garden's main axis. The model had been accepted. Baillie said Weinman was insisting on having his model enlarged by an additional ¼ or ⅛ points.[3] "That quadruples the pointing (enlarging) work. It's a waste of time," said Baillie, a Scotsman, who knew it would also quadruple costs. He was so vexed with the sculptor's stubborn attitude he couldn't work with him, and he, Baillie, had taken the liberty to farm out the enlarging job to another artist named Mazette who had a machine like Nebel's to make these fine measurements. Feeling responsible, Baillie had to tell Archer what he had done.

We do not know if he wanted Archer to reverse his decision. There is no word in Anna's diary about Archer's reaction. All she wrote was, "They are all nonsense but Weinman is a German who wants his pound of flesh." (D1944, September 13) So apparently, Archer had settled the matter by letting the sculptor have what he wanted. As things turned out, *Riders of the Dawn*, high on a pedestal in the middle of an open-work brick wall, makes a stunning, cream-colored accent in the garden.

Pursuing this portrait of a retired millionaire during wartime, we subconsciously wait for a single incident to come up showing how the national emergency interfered with Archer's life. It appears, however, that he was not inconvenienced, but contented, and actually benefited from the conditions wartime imposed. Due to gas rationing, visitors did not just drop in at Stanerigg. This allowed uninterrupted time to write in his study. He was at an age when many people look back and want to record what it was like "back then." And Archer's life had been unusually full of significant and memorable relationships and events. Essentially a modest man, he never boasted; writing a book of reminiscences was simply his way of trying to preserve what for him had distinguished his past.

After his mother died, Archer had found in her papers the detailed letters he had written to her during his Spanish travels in the 1890s. She had kept these for him as a diary of his journeys. Now he referred to these letters, and in 1943, began dictating to Miss Perkins an account of an experience he had as an archeologist in February 1898.[4]

Learning that a French archeologist was abandoning his excavations at the ruins of Roman Itálica near Seville, Archer leased the site from its owner and hired a crew to start digging. Then an odd, surprising scenario unfolded. At first they found a grave of a woman and a child. Quantities of Roman glass and pottery as well as marble sculpture were brought to light. The crew stopped, thinking that was enough, and looked at Archer. He told them to continue.

Then, to the general amazement, a workman with a pickaxe dug up a copper vessel holding what was later found to be 1,500 gold coins, two bars of silver, and one of gold. The coins filled the workman's wide-brimmed hat. Archer tried to buy the hoard, but the workman would not deal with him. "They permitted me to take a picture, examine them up close and take notes; then the law intervened in favor of the owner of the property and the government . . ." Several officials from the Commission of Monuments and the mayor of Santiponce, the village where the find was made, had gathered. They classified the coins and wanted to weigh them.

"Where are we going to do that?" asked Archer.

"The men pointed to the top of the road. We went there. The mayor was in shirtsleeves, organizing and directing the men. Through a rafter above the door, they passed a rope, which they fastened to the hook of a balance. When everything was ready, four men retired to the back room and you could hear a blood-curdling scream. Later they appeared, holding in their arms, the body of a pig, which they had tied with a heavy cord round its head and tail. What a loud pig! They hung it a moment leaving it suspended in the air while its hoggish voice gave prolonged and blood-curdling squeals of protest. After weighing it, they took it down and released it."

"Concluding the account, Archer made this enigmatic comment: 'With respect to the gold of Itálica, the most complete silence reigns.'"5

Had Anna known what Archer was working on almost every day in his study behind the closed door it is certain she would have recorded it. As it was, she only learned what he was up to when Paul Meylan, the artist who lived in a Stanerigg cottage on Old Dodgingtown Road, let the cat out of the bag. He showed Anna the sketches Archer had asked him to do, of photographs Archer had taken at the Itálica dig. (D1944, December 14) Sometimes Miss Perkins worked seven hours at a stretch and had to spend a few days at Stanerigg. "Too much at his age," objected Anna. "Besides, she's a confounded Christian Scientist. She sees so badly that her typing is full of mistakes. She will not put on glasses. She has to erase mistakes continually. It is bad for Archer, but he will not get anyone else more efficient." (D1945, November 19) Actually, Archer, who had a perverse streak, may have enjoyed watching his concerned, efficient wife squirm at how he put up with ineptitude. Regardless, the story was typed and finished and eventually given to José García-Mazas for *El Poeta*.

If closed in his office, Archer would often emerge and see a visitor whom Anna had first screened. One time the guest was Robert A. Milliken. Millikin had won the Nobel Prize for Physics in 1923, was director of the California Institute of Technology, and was currently serving as chairman of the board of the Huntington Library and Art Museum in San Marino, California. "He was insistent about visiting Archer," wrote Anna. "We suspected he must have something important to discuss or reveal about the Huntington Museum. But it happened he had nothing to discuss.

All was in the black and running smoothly in spite of income being cut to about $200,000 from $500,000. He simply talked about his discoveries about jet propulsion planes in the war effort. "Archer found him interesting. But 6 hours of talk was exhausting. They are both 74." (D1943, April 14)

Sometimes Anna's usual probity went awry, and Archer's love of good talk got him into trouble. One April day, an old ex-Connecticut senator came to call. He and Archer "drank whiskey for 3 hours before the purpose of his visit was divulged. It was to get Archer to back a scheme to put the bible (sic) on the news wire to send overseas to troops. Archer did not cooperate, and was tired out." (D1944, April 14)

Reading intently about the Huntingtons' wartime life, one finds their social habits puzzling. If these visits were so exhausting, why didn't Anna intercede by saying that snow was expected and suggest it might be prudent for a visitor to leave. It was risky having guests, for if anyone arrived on the 10:10 a.m. train, he/she would be stuck there until the afternoon train left Bethel for New York at 5:06 p.m. But for some reason the Huntingtons endured repeat visits from guests they considered "boring," even those who brought "unattractive, misbehaving" children. One particular couple who lived close enough to walk would come to tea bringing their two teenage daughters. "Why those youngsters wanted to come to see 2 old people I don't know; unless they like to look at millionaires as they would monkeys in a zoo." (D1945, September 16)

"Buried in the country," Anna and Archer were probably more lonely than they admitted. They both loved to talk and interact with people. At tea or lunch they would discuss education, Jews, the war, the price of perfume ($1000), sculpture, what FDR's teaming up with labor and communists would do for the country, the cost of nightgowns ($75) in the New York shops, the prospect of hurricane damage when Danbury power went out etc. Tired out after guests left, Anna and Archer would go to bed at 9.—late for both of them.

Wartime did, however, provide welcome contact with the outside world. Friends came to sell war bonds or solicit financial help from Archer to meet quotas, and they were never turned away. Archer and Anna always helped Bethel and Danbury meet their quotas. According to Anna, Archer bought a minimum $200,000 in war bonds. She was equally generous, though in a smaller dimension. When Archer gave $10,000 to "poor little Bethel," she gave half that. Mrs. McMahon, the judge's wife whom Anna enjoyed as a friend, got help with financing a community health care facility for children and also a generous check to equip the town with emergency vehicles that could handle fire, drownings, a fallen tree. After giving Redding a renovated fire engine brought from Rocas, Archer, the man with an obsession about making every building fireproof, was proud to be appointed Honorary Fire Chief of Redding and wear a badge. (D1942, August 19)

His generosity was unfailing. As yet, Bertram and Margaret Stroock had not come to start the Danbury Development Fund as they did in the middle 1950s, so the hospital was struggling to equip, develop and expand its facilities. Spotting the lack of a pathology lab Archer immediately gave $4000 to establish one. (D1943, December 14) He offered $50,000 to the hospital if it would match his gift. Within a few weeks, the board said they had collected over $200,000,

enough to pay off the mortgage. (D1944, June 13; July 14) The entire Danbury region was grateful that the Huntingtons, like Mark Twain, had elected to spend their older years in Redding.

If such recognition warmed Archer's cockles, another kind of attention became what Anna often called "the joy of his declining years." This was the frequent visits of the young women curators at the Hispanic Society. Archer had guided "the girls" into unexplored avenues of Spanish culture. Their first visit to the Huntingtons' home had been at Rocas; after the move to Stanerigg and the luxury of a chauffeur and car was denied them, they roughed it on the train to visit their mentor and stay for lunch.

Miss Trapier would explain the use of X-ray to date a painting by Velázquez. Mrs. Frothingham described her research into the life of the Count of Aramba who was the Spanish Ambassador to the Court of Louis XV. Most of the women had had only a secondary education, and perhaps a degree in Library Science.[6] But their work became so professional Archer raised their salaries.

After V-J Day when travel became feasible, Anna began planning a trip down to Brookgreen. She was anxious to see how Atalaya looked after its occupation during 1943 and 1944 by the 455th Bombardment Squadron from the United States Army Air Corps. Some five hundred men patrolled the beaches, fortified the grounds with machine guns, and had target practice on a temporary air field. The house on Laurel Hill which had been moved down in the 1930s, was the mess hall. Archer was equally curious, but worried that his physical condition could not tolerate the trip. Then when Anna suggested "the girls" come to visit, he cheered up and said he'd like to try

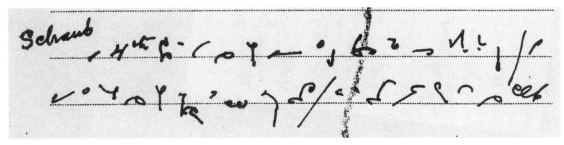

A page from Archer's notebooks. Archer was experimenting with inventing a shorthand that would be useful in any language. Anna Hyatt Huntington Papers, Syracuse University Library, Special Collections.

it.7 Archer, who had been uncertain whether he could physically tolerate the trip, felt more willing when he considered this pleasant diversion. In September, Anna made reservations at the railroad office for a private car for January 4, 1946, to leave from Bridgeport about noon, arriving the next afternoon at 3 p.m. in Georgetown, South Carolina. Archer continued to vacillate about going, which kept Anna from packing for their three-month holiday. She prayed for a severe snowstorm, something she knew would sway him to make a southern exodus. In answer to her prayer a blizzard before Christmas that "made the place look like the Adirondacks"

did come. (D1945, December 20) That, along with successful results from a new aspirin pain-relief medication, convinced Archer he wanted to go.

On January 4 all systems were "Go." Closets were locked; Annie and Miss Perkins were packed in; two maids were excited to travel in a stateroom; and Sandy, Garth's successor, "good as gold, lying quiet on his rug, held a reception from both porters on arrival at Georgetown. Archer said the trip had been like the trips he used to make with his father on the Southern Pacific. And he complimented me on managing things so well." (D1946, January 5)

1. John K. Wright. *The History of the American Geographical Society.* Published by the American Geographical Society. 1952. 145.

2. *Brookgreen Gardens.* Wyrick & Company. Charleston, S.C. 1999. Photographs and Text. 16.

3. David Gesualdi, sculptor in Bethel, Connecticut, telephone interview with Albert Goodrich, September 2, 2003. David explains what the fractions mean. The enlarging machine works on the principle of the pantograph. Baillie is directing the probe. "At the beginning the turntables, which are chained together, are locked in position. A starts drilling at the top of the stone until Baillie's probe touches the model. Then R withdraws the drill and moves it further down a fixed amount vertically and drills another hole until Baillie's probe strikes the model again etc., etc. When R gets to the bottom, they turn the turntables a small angle, lock them and start over at the top. A.A. Weinman was insisting the vertical motion be ¼″ or ⅛″. It may be justified for fine details as a face or hands but not for the large, gently contoured surfaces comprising much of the *Riders of the Dawn.*"

4. Gerald J. MacDonald to Mary Mitchell, 5 June 2003.

5. G-M. *El Poeta.* 395–415.

6. Gerald J. MacDonald, inteviewed by Mary Mitchell. 5 June 2003.

7. *Visitor's Guide,* 14, 15

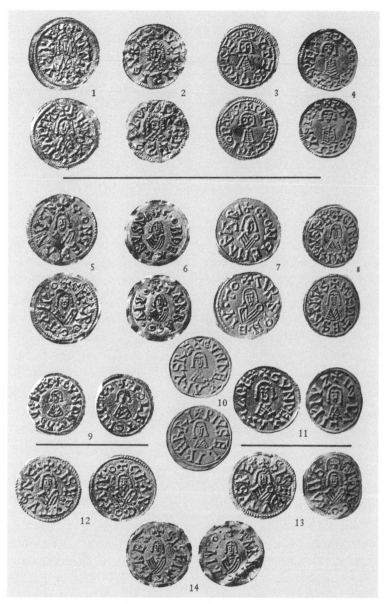

Visigothic coins minted in the reigns of Kings Witteric, Gundemar, and Sisebut, 603–621 A.D. Plate-VIII. *The Coinage of the Visigoths of Spain Leovigild to Achila II.* George C. Miles. American Numismatic Society. New York. 1952. Dr. Miles found these coins to have been minted in Baelica or the Andalucia of today.

CHAPTER 13

ARCHER, COINS, AND THE VISIGOTHS

1946–1947

IN THE SPRING OF 1946, after returning from Brookgreen, Archer started what became a massive enterprise. Batch by batch, he transferred his collection of 30,355 ancient coins to the American Numismatic Society from the Hispanic Society next door on Audubon Terrace. On each trip Anna accompanied him.

Archer began collecting coins as a boy, and pursued this interest as a youth on his journey though northern Spain in the 1890s. His vast collection had been resting in heavy steel vaults in the cellar of the Hispanic Society since the building opened for use in 1908. In his methodical, determined way, Archer traveled with Anna from Stanerigg to New York every two or three weeks to make the transfers. At these times they stayed at No. 1 East Eighty-ninth Street, their city perch.

The routine was always the same. Each batch, numbering anywhere from 300 to 3000 coins, had to be listed and photographed by curators, Archer's young women protégées learning archival techniques. Archer, and only Archer, would go down to the cellar and bring up the batch of the day in a leather bag or steel case to the packing room and supervise what was done. Then he, himself, would carry the bag or trundle the case in a cart or wheelbarrow to the American Numismatic Society. By mutual agreement, the Society had custody of them on indefinite loan.

At first, its president, Dr. Herbert E. Ives, was so impatient to get the collection into his building and under his jurisdiction, he grew angry with Archer's deliberate methods. But Archer was stubborn. Things had to be done his way, or the deal was off. Ives (1882–1953) had just retired from Bell Telephone Laboratories as an optical physicist, and was used to calling the shots. But in this case, he realized he must contain himself and wait. (D1946, May 10) By November 1947 the enterprise was completed.

During this time, Dr. Ives introduced Archer to Capt. George C. Miles, still in uniform as a captain in Army Intelligence. (D1946, May 7) Dr. Miles (1904–1975) had graduated from Princeton in 1926 with a Ph.D. in ancient Persian and Arabic coins.[1] Archer realized here was the man he had been looking for to catalog his collection, and offered him $5000 a year for ten years, three-month's vacation, and publication of his books. His offer was accepted and in June of 1946, Miles commenced to work in the Numismatic building.

Corner of a tray of Visigothic coins in a vault at the American Numismatic Society at 140 William Street, New York. Credit, A. S. Goodrich.

In his book, *The Coinage of the Visigoths*, published six years later, Miles conveys the historic and cultural significance of coins. And he describes how during Archer's travels in northern Spain in 1890–1891, he heard about the La Capilla hoard of Visigothic coins found in a town eighteen miles northeast of Seville. It numbered somewhere between 800 and 1000 coins.

"A construction worker was digging at the foundations of a wall near the La Capilla farmhouse, on the property of General José Chincilla," writes Dr. Miles. "At a depth of 25 centimeters (a centimeter = 0.39 inch) the workman's pick shattered an earthenware pot containing a large quantity of what were later identified as Visigothic coins. The bulk of the hoard was sold by the workmen to a merchant in Seville while some 250 specimens were commandeered by General Chincilla."[2] It is unclear how Archer acquired the hoard. But it constituted the most important part of his huge final collection of Iberian coins dating back to the Roman, Carthaginian, Islamic, mediaeval Spanish, and Christian eras.

Made of pure gold, the La Capilla coins are about the size and thickness of a dime or a nickel. Even after some 1500 years in the earthenware pot, they are in shining mint-new condition. Secured now in three corridor-like, fireproof vaults at the Society, each coin is set in its tiny, custom-made box, numbered and identified, and stored in trays, one above the other. A sense of antiquity emanates from the very sight and feel under the thumb of this thin gold disk. In Visigothic Spain, one coin might buy a horse, so the curator says. A handful might reward a victorious general. In those times there were no banks or hotel vaults or storage facilities to hold one's money. So army officers, landlords, and royalty packed their moneys or coins on their travels with all the other necessary baggage. Then if a battle erupted, or there was a landslide, a life-threatening flood, or a sudden enemy attack, the hoard was dumped into the handiest vessel and buried. The person who had hidden it might be killed, taken prisoner, or die. So there it would lie hidden for centuries, only coming to light in the way the La Capilla hoard did. In the history of coin-collecting such discoveries are not uncommon, as Archer discovered when he started buying up other collections during his travels in Spain.

In the early 1900s, after returning from Spain and while constructing the Hispanic Society building, he heard about a society in New York founded in 1858 and devoted to numismatics. He joined it in 1899. "As its president from 1905 to 1910, Archer Huntington played a big part in constructing and financing the present American Numismatic Society next to the Hispanic building on Audubon Terrace. With his vision and force as well as his material resources it was built into a great institution."3

But it wasn't until he was in his late 70s, gradually shedding responsibilities of all kinds, that Archer felt like placing his collection in the American Numismatic Society. Why he waited so long is unclear. Perhaps it was because he was waiting to find a scholar, the likes of George Miles, meeting his high standards to catalog the collection.

And who indeed were the Visigoths? James Michener in his book, *Iberia*, tells us. "The first Germanic tribes that spilled over into Spain after the debacle of the Roman Empire were mere barbarian vandals. They left no mark on the Spanish population and were so disorganized that it was relatively easy for the superior Visigoths to supersede them. Establishing a kingdom in central Spain with a capital at Toledo, they had kings with strange, un-Spanish names like Leovigild, Tulga, and Reccared, who ruled Iberia from 568 to 711 AD, thus accounting for the blue-eyed Spaniards one sees there occasionally."4 Surprisingly, King Reccared was a Christian and, in 589, pledged allegience to the Catholic Church of Rome, the most prized Visigothic heritage to the Spain of the future. The Visigoths may have left no legacy of literature or art or architecture, but they were law-givers and developed a system of coinage out of necessity. They taxed the landholders and to consolidate their kingdom fought battles with rebellious Gothic nobles. So property-owners had to have coins to pay taxes and warlords had to pay soldiers and reward generals.

For a long time minting in Spain was a busy industry. Along the streams and rivulets of the mountains in southern and western Iberia were rich alluvial deposits of gold, silver and copper. In his studies of the Visigothic hoard, Miles met with seventy-nine mint names embossed on the coins. Many mints were located in Galicia along the riverbeds north of what is now Portugal,[5] and more in what is now Andalucia where Seville, Cordoba and Granada are located. To identify precisely where the La Capilla coins were struck, Miles took soil samples from each Iberian province. He then matched these samples with the traces of soil still encrusted on the La Capilla coins.[6] Baetica, which is today's Andalucia, with streams threading down through the Sierra Nevada to the Mediterranean Sea, proved to be the area where the La Capilla coins were minted.

In addition, Miles wanted to know when the coins were struck. A study of each coin's legend revealed this. Scrutinizing the inscription images of both sides of the coins under a microscope, he was able to discern the names of the kings in whose reign the coin was struck. The kings were Sisebut, Suinthila, and Sisenand who ruled one after the other in the middle 600s A.D.[7]

George Miles was doing for Archer Huntington what the aging bibliophile had, himself, wanted to do but never had the time to do it. Archer had begun collecting coins at about age nine, and in his own words, "It was perhaps ten years before I perceived what responsibilities I had assumed. When I started to print a catalogue of acquired material I became aware of the fact that I had been little more than a mere collector and that I was faced with the consideration of backgrounds of history, science and art with which I was not sufficiently equipped at the time."[8]

Archer delivered the last batch of coins to the American Numismatic Society on November 7, 1947. The president of the Numismatic Society, Dr. Ives, had died that year, and Princeton professor Louis G. West succeeded him. He and Archer got along famously. A fine administrator, Dr. West kept his eye on the bottom line. Appreciating that, Archer gave the society large sums whenever Dr. West told him what was needed. During the next two years, Archer gave the society a total of $165,000 to improve display arrangements for the society's collections of medals and coins, and to enlarge exhibit rooms and the reading room on the first floor.[9]

While under Archer's employ, Dr. Miles wrote and had published two books about the coins. The first, *The Coinage of the Umayyads of Spain*, was published in 1950. Constituting the western branch of the Arab caliphate, the Umayyads were a Muslim dynasty who invaded southern Spain and, in the late 700s, vanquished the Visigoths. They minted their own coinage.

On October 20, 1952, Dr. Miles visited Stanerigg to present Archer with his last book, *The Coinage of the Visigoths*. Anna wrote that Archer was pleased to read the dedication, which is "Archer Milton Huntington—Humanist, Scholar, and Poet."

A year later, in an extraordinary effort to show his interest in how the society was getting along, Archer went with Anna, "taking the back way, climbed up the back stairs, 3 long flights, to see the new rooms and the impressive way coins were preserved." (D1953, October 7) Archer was 83 years old, Anna, 77.

* * *

SATISFYING as the completed task may have been to Archer, the effort involved in keeping to his schedule and making sure each batch of coins delivered was recorded accurately, took its toll on his usually calm, well-balanced nervous system. Always conscious of being the custodian of a great fortune, about halfway through the transfer, he grew anxious about the safety of his bank deposits. Viscerally unable to trust his securities, stocks, and bonds, his records, and important documents to a single or even two banks, he had distributed the entire corpus among six banks, namely J. P. Morgan & Co., the New York Trust Company, the Guaranty Trust Company, the Central Hanover Bank, the Chemical Bank, and the Bankers Trust Company. Bonds with coupons, for example, were kept at Guaranty Trust, Chemical, and Central Hanover. Land deeds and trust documents were with Bankers Trust, coupon-bonds with Chemical, and so on.

Taking advantage of being in New York on a coin-delivery journey, he and Anna would go to a bank to do business. They would spend a second night or an afternoon reviewing securities or cutting coupons. There were no notes to worry about, for Archer's unbroken policy was never to lend money. Impatient to finish and tired, if he couldn't find the document or if the lock to the safety deposit box didn't work, he grew suspicious. He was sure the box had been tampered with, deliberately damaged, or the document stolen. (D1947, April 9; March 13) He would then call for a clerk to get a hacksaw to open the box. Sometimes he would feel so uneasy about boxes in one bank where he thought something had been stolen, and with Anna's help, move them to another. Inevitably, in the switch, one would be lost or mis-

placed. After a sleepless night, he would decide to stay over yet another night to look again for it the next day. Just as inevitably, Anna would return to the first bank, and find the document misplaced in transit. "His imagination takes over," wrote Anna, "and destroys his sleep, and if he's taken home a list for Miss Perkins to copy and finds a document missing, he blames poor myopic Perkins for the loss. Then I find it, and he has to apologize to her." (D1947, February 18) He was the same way about keys to his various boxes. If he couldn't find the right one, he was sure it was lost, and back at home, he would have copies made at the Bethel Hardware Store. Then, of course, Anna would find the heavy keyring under papers on his desk.

Sometimes, these petty annoyances made him perverse. "When Mr. Johnson of the Bankers Trust came to see him and insist that he convert many of his taxable bonds to state non-taxable bonds to save a lot of taxes and have more coupon income, Archer let him finish his spiel, then calmly stated he did not want any more income. It was fine as it was. The poor fellow could not fathom such an attitude, and left, having failed completely in his mission." (D1948, January 16)

However, there were compensations. The Bankers Trust made out their income tax returns. In opening his box at Guaranty Trust Archer admitted there could not have been tampering, for he found there a lot of loose cash that he said must have been there for at least thirty years. (D1953, October 6) These aberrations on Archer's part only lasted for the period when he was transferring his coin collection. After the strain of that chore was gone, we do not find any more incidents recorded of frayed nerves and suspicions about having his papers tampered with.

While fleshing out the picture of Archer and his obsession with security, there is one more story to tell. When the lawyers probating Archer's estate made the inventory of his tangible personal property, they went down into the basement of Stanerigg to look around. "There were two safes for which the combinations could not be found," said Thomas L. Cheney. "It was assumed they were full of gold bars or Treasury bonds. The safe-opener had to tip them on their face and burn a hole through the back with a torch. They both contained shotgun ammunition. In addition, we found a walk-in vault containing 4 4-drawer filing cabinets. Each drawer had its own lock and combination and in each drawer were two leather-bound boxes, each with a lock. Nothing worthwhile was in any of the leather-bound boxes." When the safes and the vault were installed in the Stanerigg basement, is unclear. Anna never mentions them. Perhaps Archer had them set there as a backup storage facility in case he lost trust in his banks. Archer was "lock-happy."[10]

1. *Who Was Who in America.* V. 6. (1974–1976). 283.

2. George C. Miles, *The Coinage of the Visigoths of Spain: Leovigild to Achila II.* Published in cooperation with the Hispanic Society of America and the American Numismatic Society. New York. 1952. Dedicated to Archer Milton Huntington—Humanist—Scholar—Poet. 25, 74. 166ff.

3. Howard L. Adelson. *The American Numismatic Society 1858–1958.* New York. The American Numismatic Society. 1958. 348.

4. James Michener, *Iberia: Spanish Travels and Reflections.* Random House. 1968. 101f.

5. Miles. 74.

6. Ibid., 75f.

7. Ibid., 74.

8. Adleson. 278.

9. $165,000, total given by AMH. D1952, February 10; April 17, December 15; D1953, October 7.

10. Thomas L. Cheney to MM. 1 October 2001.

CHAPTER 14

ANNA, HORSES, AND A CUBAN JOURNALIST
1946–1954

ONE DAY, WHILE ANNA was with Archer in New York delivering coins, she took time out to visit her old haunts in Greenwich Village. "I didn't know a soul," she wrote in her diary. "I felt like a fish out of water." (D1946, May 15) This feeling sparked her creative instincts, lying fallow for six or more years. After finishing *Boabdil*, she had said she would never do another large piece. Yet here she was, wire tool in hand, involving herself again, with the irresistible urge compelling her fingers to start a second *Don Quixote*.

In her studio she found the plaster cast of Rocinante that had been used for the first *Don* in 1942, and called Nebel, the sculptor who had the enlarging machine, to pick it up, make a half-size model and return it to her. While he was doing this, she started a small clay sketch model, about 8 or 9 inches high, portraying a new version of the *Don* that had intrigued her for a long time. The first one had shown the Don as he set out on his mission. Now she wanted to show him on his return to La Mancha, bent and frail, after his disastrous encounter with the windmill, yet still looking ahead with an optimism his recent failures had not extinguished.[1]

This version had come to her through a happy coincidence. She had noticed Lester Nicholson, her old Scottish gardener, bent and thin, working in the rosebed near the studio where he had worked ever since the beginning of World War II. (D1946, October 1) Suddenly, the similarity between him and the Don, both stooped and thin with age, yet both determined and undefeated, struck her. A more practical thought occurred to her. Here at hand, available every day, was a model for the Don. Whenever she needed to, she could take his measurements, study his posture, put him on a horse, and the statue would quickly take shape.

All summer, in between journeys into the city with Archer, handling farm matters, seeing friends or walking dogs, she would enter the studio to work on the model. Working fast so as not to lose the image in her mind, putting clothes and armor on the Don's body, she wrote, "I'm having much fun with this." (D1946, August 8) Her excitement carried her through until she had finished a one-quarter size working model of the Don and called Contini to come and see it.

When he came and walked around the figure, he was excited. "My God! My God! What work! You do better as you get older!" (D1946, October 1) Three

119

weeks later, after making the mold, he returned, plaster in hand, made the cast and took it away to deliver to Nebel. Nebel was the sculptor who would make the half-size enlargement in clay, on which Anna would make corrections and add further detail.

Nebel and Contini had become essential to Anna. Cesare (pronounced *Chay*sarray) Contini was a fifth-generation plaster caster and a master at his craft. The first two generations worked in Rome and the Vatican doing piece molds. "For some obscure religious reason my grandfather was ordered to leave Rome," he told George Gurney, an interviewer for the Smithsonian Institution's *Archives of American Art*. "He moved to Naples. In the 1890s, his son, my uncle, had emigrated to New York and worked on buildings for the World's Fair of 1893. He was so busy he asked my father, Attilio, to come over and help out. Father liked New York so well he sent for my mother whom he had been courting. She came and they were married. I was born there, in Greenwich Village. Around 1920 when I was about ten, he began to work in the studio of James Earle Fraser, a famous sculptor. In the 1930s Fraser had contracts to do sculpture for the Federal Triangle buldings like the Department of Commerce, the Archives, Supreme Court, and Justice etc. I worked in Fraser's studio too, and that's how I came to cast the work of his wife, Laura Gardin Fraser, in the 1940s and 50s. She and Mrs. Huntington were close friends, and she introduced me to Mrs. Huntington."[2]

Anna once asked him if he intended to keep on with casting, and he said yes. "I said I would stop modeling if he went out of business as there are no other casters I want to do my work." (D1952, August 29) Cesare married and had a home and studio at 340

Anna touching up the neck of *Don Quixote II* in 1949. Her model for the Don was Lester Nicholson, Stanerigg's longtime Scottish gardener. His daily presence around the place was convenient for her. Any time she had to remeasure the Don's leg or shoulder, she could just call Nicholson into the studio, put him on the horse, and make the change. Courtesy, Anna Hyatt Huntington Papers, Syracuse University Library, Special Collections.

West 12th Street in the Village. He and his father ran the business called Attilio J. Contini & Sons.

Nebel's background was described earlier.[3] In addition to being a good sculptor he took jobs enlarging or reducing sculpture not only because he had the proper machine but also because he needed

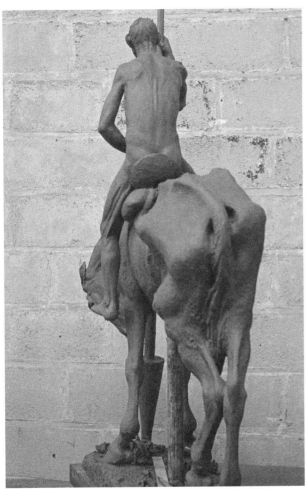

Don Quixote's horse, *Rocinante*, at the end of the Don's journeys. Émile Schaub-Koch. *L'œuvres d'Anna Hyatt Huntington*. Editions Messein. 1949. 344. Photograph by Lucia Nebel White.

The *Don* and *Sancho Panza*, the Don's faithful companion. Anna did the Don and Paul Jennewein, the Sancho Panza. Brookgreen Gardens. Credit, A. S. Goodrich.

the money. His daughter, Lucia Nebel White, told us he had one machine he used only for Anna's work. Nebel took the *Quixote* cast, but didn't return it for Anna to start revising until March of 1947.

Immediately, she noticed a number of major cor-rections to do. First, she stripped off the stirrups to redo them. Then the head had to be taken off and enlarged separately so that she could work on it to better advantage. The cloak needed a rougher tex-ture so it would stand out from the figure. Noticing that the left thigh was too long, she had to remeasure Nicholson's leg. The tip of the lance had to be reworked to show damage from the Don's encounter with the windmill. The head which Nebel had enlarged so she could work on it to better advantage, had to come off again and be reattached at a better angle. While doing this, Anna had the chance to shorten the neck. These adjustments took over six months.

Delays were due to three reasons. Both Nebel and Contini had other clients, and Anna's work had to wait its turn. Then Contini needed help with handling the fragile, heavy group and couldn't always get it when necessary. In addition, Anna's life had many interruptions. A trip with Archer into town "took out a week when I cannot do anything. People are coming thick and fast. The Duchess of Montoro, the Duke of Alba's daughter, is here, staying at the Waldorf, and we must entertain her at lunch and dinner which Sherry's will cater. Curators from the Huntington Museum in San Marino, California, are here too. Time to work is scarce." (D1947, April 18)

Still another delay held up the *Don*. When she thought it was finished, she had had Contini take it to a foundry for casting in bronze. In April of 1948 the foundry went bankrupt, and the pieces had to be transferred from temporary storage to another foundry. (D1948, December 5) At last, by April of 1949, after having Archer's lawyer resolve many troublesome problems, Anna was able to settle "my poor old Q" at Roman Bronze, the foundry in Corona, New York, in Queens, with whom she had done business when working on the first *El Cid*. (D1949, April 5) Casting each piece separately, the Roman Bronze artisans reassembled the statue, and by early 1950 Anna's poor old man and his horse had found their place at Brookgreen Gardens. (D1949, October 31)

To complete the story: Subsequently, Brookgreen had Paul Jennewein, a highly respected sculptor, do a statue of Sancho Panza, the Don's loyal attendant, to stand behind Anna's splendid *Quixote* in the Gardens.[4] A plaque on a pedestal near the statue tells how Jennewein used himself as a model for Sancho Panza by means of a mirror beside the donkey.

* * *

THE WORKING RELATIONSHIP between Anna, Contini, and Nebel reached a peak of perfection during the three and a half years it took to produce the *Fighting Stallions*. Here are two magnificent antagonists in a moment of fierce, overpowering emotion. The attacking horse clamps his teeth into the other's vulnerable neck as the weaker horse flings up his head in agony and despair at his inevitable defeat. Implicit in the group is Anna's mastery of her craft.

In her diary Anna rarely wrote about a sculpture she might be planning. Nor did she tell anyone what she might be thinking about. Inside her head there lay a kind of artistic nest, a secret place no one else had access to, where a sculpture would be born, evolve, and then like a baby bird in its shell, abruptly emerge, ready to grow.

So it was that on August 5, 1947, while waiting for Nebel to bring back Rocinante's hind legs for her to rework, there suddenly appeared the entry, "Started group of fighting stallions." Excited and working fast so she wouldn't lose the image she envisioned, five days later she showed it to her neighbor who had been a rancher in the West. He said he hadn't ever seen stallions fight in just that position, but that it looked right to him. "I'm glad I got it right," she wrote, "for I had never seen a fight." (D1947, August 10)

Reassured, she was ready in ten days for Contini to come, make a mold of the sketch model and then the plaster cast. He took it to Nebel who in two months brought Anna a clay enlargement for her to work on. She made a number of changes, trying to finish this first effort because Archer wanted her to go with him to New York in a few days. By the end of January 1948, Contini came again to cast a "small fighting stallions," which he delivered to Nebel to enlarge to ¼ life-size. (D1947, December 2) "Nebel could only enlarge from a hard surface like plaster," said Elisabeth Gordon Chandler.[5] Knowing this would happen, Anna welcomed the chance to correct, change, and add detail as she saw her original idea develop and gain conviction.

Moving from ¼ to ½ life-size was the next phase and a big jump. At this point the statue was sizeable, and in order for Anna to work effectively, the body-parts of each horse had to be detached from one another and cast separately. Since Contini was to do the separating, Nebel came up from his home in Westport to meet him at Anna's studio and indicate where to cut for enlarging. (D1948, August 30)

As usual, frustrating delays intervened. With so many individual pieces to be cast, then enlarged in clay by Nebel, the half-size model wasn't ready for Anna's review until October 1949. By then Contini and Nebel had set up a platform in the studio, placed on it the bodies of the horses in their proper relation to each other, and attached each body-part correctly so that Anna could look at the group as a whole. Having the parts brought to her studio and assembled there was expensive. But Anna was not hard up and needed every hour at home or with Archer. She couldn't spend time driving here and there if it could be avoided. When Nebel and Contini called her to come look at the assembled group in the studio she

Fighting Stallions, 1950, one of Anna's major sculptures, is fifteen feet high, made of aluminum, and stands at the entrance to Brookgreen Gardens, South Carolina, on U.S. Route 17. Credit, Paul Hoffmann.

must have been pleased, for she brought out a bottle of wine and some cake for all to clink glasses and toast their joint achievement. (D1948, April 11)

Contini's bill to date was $1100. He said that the foundry's charge for casting *Fighting Stallions* would be $11,000. "An awful price but can't be helped," commented Anna. (D1948, October 8, 22) Having Contini cast it, piece by piece, before delivery to

Archer's *Memorial* to his mother, Arabella Huntington. Anna created the first model in 1948, and the group was finished in 1951 by Robert Baillie, stonecarver and sculptor. Archer wrote the poem on the base. The memorial stands on the Collis P. Huntington lot at Woodlawn Cemetery in the Bronx, New York, near the mausoleum Collis built in 1883. Arabella is not interred here, but in the mausoleum she and her second husband, Henry Edwards Huntington, built at The Huntington Library and Art Collections in San Marino, California.

Roman Bronze was also costly. Anna knew how to do it herself, for she had been sculpting monumental figures for over fifty years. But Contini's help saved her time and cleaning up a mess. Moreover, with him in charge, she had peace of mind. Nothing phased him.

After Anna gave the green light, Contini and his son took the group down from the platform, disassembled it, and then made a plaster cast of each part in the studio, a tremendous job that lasted twelve days. Each of the twenty-six pieces was laid carefully on the floor where they remained until April 10, 1950, when Contini and the driver from the foundry spent six hours loading them onto the Roman Bronze truck. The foundry cast the parts separately in aluminum and then assembled them into the final group.

The foundry estimated a value of $21,000 each for the two *Fighting Stallions* they cast, one intended for Brookgreen Gardens and the other, a smaller one, for a Redding Public School. (D1950, January 20) Contini insured the horses for $20,000, and the insurance company required him to ride beside the driver to keep him from reckless driving and to see that he did not take any liquor while driving. (D1950, April 10) The truck left at 2:30 p.m. Contini was beside the driver. After successful delivery, the plaster caster received his last payment of $4000. (D1950, April 24; November 28)

By early 1951, *Fighting Stallions* was ready to be shipped to Brookgreen. By the first of the year Frank Tarbox received the shipment and after uncrating the group, placed it in the Palm Garden. Years later, it was moved out to the entrance into the Gardens on U. S. Route 17 where it stands today, a brilliant, eye-catching landmark.

* * *

NO STRANGER TO HARD WORK, Anna hated to be idle. It was not unusual for a *Godiva* to stand unfinished and waiting for her fingers beside a *Fish-*

erman's Fountain and a *Displaced Woman*, all ready for Contini to come and cast them. So it was in this setting that Anna, in July of 1948, when the *Quixote* was at the foundry and the horses were with Nebel, started a sketch model of a sculpture Archer had asked her to do. (D1948, July 8, 9) It was a memorial to his mother, Arabella Huntington, that was to be placed in the Collis P. Huntington plot at Woodlawn Cemetery near Throgg's Neck in the Bronx. In 1883 Collis's first wife, Elizabeth, died. Needing a place to inter her with dignity and due respect, he bought a plot of four lots in the cemetery and on it built a mausoleum patterned after a Roman temple.[6] Eventually, Elizabeth was interred there, also Catherine Yarrington, Arabella's mother, and Collis himself. Arabella is not there. She is in the mausoleum she and her second husband, Henry E. Huntington, built for themselves on his "ranch" at San Marino, California, where the renowned Huntington Library and Art Collections now is. But Archer wanted a memorial to his mother placed near his father, her first husband, and near where he himself would be some day.

For the memorial Anna designed a life-sized figure of a tall matronly woman wearing a hooded cape and stretching out her arms to embrace a young male and a young female, both nude, seated side-by-side. He looks down pensively. She smiles up at the "madre," and the "madre" smiles down at her. Between the two young people is a cornucopia spilling out fruit and books. The whole backs up against a huge cross whose bold and simple shape sets off the complex design in front.

Once the sketch met Archer's approval, he and Anna, Robert Baillie, a stone carver, and the ceme-tery engineer met at the Woodlawn site. After studying the model Anna had brought, Baillie said he would need a block of limestone measuring 10′ x 8′, weighing 30 tons. (D1949, February 3) The engineer said he would dig a hole the proper size and depth, and Archer told him to go down to bedrock if necessary. The memorial would be heavy.

Time had to pass while Anna had cataract surgery in November 1948. (D1948, November 16) Two months later, in January, she started to work on the model, finding it "the devil trying to mold with one eye. Everything looks flat. You can't see or measure. Don't know if I can finish this piece or not—perhaps doing a drape will be easier." (D1949, January 5) Two days later, she tried again. "It's desperately hard, may make a mess of it—should have a large space of glass to work with—am using trifocals not good for work." Two more months had to pass before her vision was normal. Then in one intense week, she finished the fruit, then the madre's bust, had Lucia come to photograph the model, and called Contini to make the mold and take it to his studio to cast. She told him to contact Baillie about when to pick up the cast.

At this point the story grows fuzzy. Baillie seems to be in charge. He is, after all, an experienced stone carver. There are no notes that Anna planned to carve the 30-ton block herself when it arrived. With Baillie coming to Archer for approval to set the memorial on the Huntington plot, the likelihood then is that Anna had turned the production over to Baillie. When the stone arrived at his workshop in Closter, New Jersey, he was to carve it, using the cast Contini had given him as a model. "It is very usual," commented Elisabeth Gordon Chandler, "for busy sculptors to leave most, if not all of the work, to the carver who does it with a 3-point compass or an enlarging/carving machine. Baillie also would have had a place to dispose of the excess stone."[7]

When it was placed on the Huntington plot at Woodlawn is unclear, but it was sometime in 1951. Although Woodlawn seems to have no record of placing the Arabella Huntington monument in the Huntington plot, a letter from Harriet Hyatt Mayor, Anna's devoted sister, dated June 11, 1952, tells how she drove past the Huntington site to see the memorial and reported that shrubs set it off beautifully.[8] Incised on the base-slab was the word "MADRE", and under it, Archer's verse:

ALAS, WE KNOW YOUR DEEDS; YOUR WORDS
MAKE WARM THE MEMORY OF OUR LOSS;
SO, IN THE NIGHT WE, DREAMING, FIND
THE DARK IN STARLIGHT'S SPELL AND KNOW
THAT FROM YOUR EYES THAT STARLIGHT FELL.

* * *

THE *Torch Bearer*, the fourth major piece of this period, was born out of fear for the nation's future, a fear shared by both Anna and Archer. In this allegorical group a male equestrian reaches down to take a lighted torch from the outstretched hand of a youth prostrate on the rocky ground. The concept Anna had in mind was that one generation will pass on to the next "the finer things in life that lead to Peace."[9]

It was spring 1950. The North Korean army supported by the Soviets was moving aggressively across the 38th parallel into South Korea. The dread circumstances of war, still vivid from living through the last one, depressed both Huntingtons. "Could be the spark of another world war," said Archer. "And this time we will not be on the sidelines but in it up to our necks." (D1950, June 26) On March 10 Anna had staged a family luncheon catered by Sherry's to celebrate Archer's 80th birthday. Balloons and limericks by Brantz Mayor enhanced the feast. But the euphoria Archer had felt during this gala event evaporated as the sobering war news came in over the radio.

Compounding their anxieties were stories coming from artistic circles in New York that Communists were infiltrating art organizations, trying to take over American art education and art societies. The president of the National Academy of Design at the time was DeWitt M. Lockman, a onetime schoolmate of Archer's. Lunching with Anna and Archer after taking office, Lockman said his foremost aim was to "get the Reds out of the governing board." (D1949, May 20) Archer backed him in his fight with a $200,000 check for a "publication fund as one way to fight." (D1949, May 29) Two months later, when he heard that a certain group of Reds "were crazy to get their hands on that money," Archer told Lockman to spend as much capital as he could while in office. (D1950, February 8) Archer's uncharacteristically rash attitude shows how uneasy he felt about the situation in an institution he had liberally supported for many years. (It was also the institution to which ten years earlier Archer had given his former home at 1083 Fifth Avenue.)

The war so affected Anna that she turned to the medium she knew best, sculpture, to express her own anxieties. As Susan Edwards wrote in her enlightening thesis about Anna's work: "Huntington created this piece after the Korean conflict when the horrors of war and maturity had mellowed the aging traditionalist."[10] Working feverishly every day in the summer on a small clay model to show the statue's

126

composition, she called Contini to cast and deliver it to Nebel for a one-quarter-sized enlargement. Eight months passed before she had it back in her studio to work on. Since Contini was busy with another client, a colleague named Petscu made a second mold after she had made her revisions, then cast it and delivered it to Nebel for enlarging to one-half life-size. On December first of 1950 Nebel brought the enlargement. With no 1951 diary to read, we are left in the dark as to what happened next.

By early 1951 a cease-fire for the Korean war was negotiated; peace was declared, and Anna's anxieties cooled down. Apprehensive, fearing *Torch* had been finished and sent somewhere else, we opened the 1952 diary. Behold, there it was, the one-half-sized model still standing in the studio corner. With no specific destination for *Torch* in mind, and also knowing that Brookgreen Gardens would always have a place for it, she had put the group aside and was busy with a statue of *Godiva* and a *Fisherman's Fountain*. (*Torch* was made of plastcline, a substance that is made from clay with some type of oil added, so it was not cracked and did not not dry out like water clay, which does dry out if not kept damp.)[11]

For twenty months *Torch* once more "began and ceased, and then again began."[12] In August of 1952 Anna wrote she had finished working on the half-life-sized group. Busy in a studio cluttered with unfinished pieces, she must have decided to finish up "the man and the horse," for she asked Nebel to estimate the cost of enlarging it to full-size. He told Anna that the group would be nine feet high, and cost between eight and nine thousand dollars. (D1952, September 2) Encouraged, Anna had her studio cleaned and rearranged to accommodate a group nine feet high. It was December 26, 1952, and she expected it any day.

It wasn't until April of '53, however, that things began to happen. Nebel brought the enlarged forelegs of the torch bearer's horse, then a month later, the head of the horse. Three more months and the studio grew more crowded as Contini appeared to rig up a hoist with steel cables. Twice more Nebel came, first, with the hindquarters of the horse and on October 24, with the last section of the group.

Then, two days later, there occurred a catalytic event, which eventually gave *Torch* a destination and a purpose. A Cuban journalist named José García-Mazas came to see Archer to interview him for an article to appear in a chain of Spanish newspapers. (D1953, October 26) Born in 1912, Mazas had degrees from the Universities of Valencia and Madrid; he had become an American citizen in 1946. Currently, he was teaching Spanish at New York University.[13] Pleased at the attention and the chance to converse in Spanish, Archer agreed to a date ten days later. After the interview, Mazas wrote the article, had it published, and soon informed Archer he was receiving congratulatory letters from all over Spain. (D1954, January 19)

In the next months, as Mazas continued to visit Stanerigg, it was inevitable that Anna should show him the *Torch Bearer*, now an impressive group nine feet high, standing up in the center of the cluttered studio, virtually complete with all its parts assembled. She told Mazas its message. We do not know what the sequence was, for it was the Christmas holidays and Anna did not write anything in her diary. But the fact was that on January 16, 1954, there appeared the surprising entry that she had offered

The *Torch Bearer*, an allegorical sculpture, was created in Spring 1950 as the Korean War threatened world peace. To express her anxiety Anna created a sculpture conveying the concept that one generation will pass onto the next the finer things in life that lead to Peace. Archer's Cuban friend, José García-Mazas, persuaded Anna to offer the group to the University of Madrid. He stands by the statue as it is hoisted into place in Madrid before the College of Medicine on May 17, 1955. Archer had given him $5000 to go to Madrid and represent him and Anna at the dedication. Courtesy, Anna Hyatt Huntington Papers, Syracuse University Library, Special Collections.

Anna gave Cuba a replica of *Torch Bearer*. The Batista government was so pleased that it asked Anna to create a statue of *José Martí*, a Cuban patriot. The result was a statue showing Martí the very moment on May 19, 1895, when he was killed in a battle for Cuban independence. When the Cubans in New York viewed the statue in her studio, they said the head was too big. So Anna took it off to reduce it. Here she poses for Brantz Mayor, her nephew, to photograph her beside the head and under the left rear leg of the horse. (We do not know if this is the first or the reduced head.) The statue stands in Central Park, New York. Courtesy, Anna Hyatt Huntington Papers, Syracuse University Library, Special Collections.

Torch to the University of Madrid. So we must conclude that Mazas, a man of culture, resource, and imagination, was responsible for Anna's felicitous move. Within a fortnight Sanchez Bella, mayor of Madrid, cabled her: "We accept your offer with the greatest pleasure. The statue will stand in front of the College of Medicine." Anna then tells how Mazas "hugged himself with joy that he has brought about this gift to Spain." (D1954, February 1)

For two months *Torch* stood like a monolith on the scaffold for viewing. Anna's nephew, Brantz Mayor, came with his wife, Ana, and their family of five children; a Redding High School class showed up too. In March, preparing for shipment to Roman Bronze, Contini came to take the group apart, ending up with over thirty pieces. When he finished, Anna asked him to pick up a piece and sign his name on it as 'plaster caster.' "He was very pleased, saying it was the first time he had been asked to do this on any sculpture." (D1954, March 24)

While Anna dealt with Contini in her studio, Archer remained aloof. Hoarding his energies, he usually left matters to Anna. But since the plans for *Torch* had come about due to his lifelong interest in Spain, he wanted to participate. Asking Contini to come to his office, he paid the husky artisan in his plaster-spotted overalls the $6000 bill for his fine work. (D1954, April 8) When the Roman Bronze foundry had completed its work and loaded the pieces, Anna learned that the statue was insured for $30,000. (D1954, March 25)

On April 8, 1955, it was trucked to Jersey City for shipment on Export Lines to Barcelona. Anna listed expenses. Boxing the nine-foot statue in a crate that measured 16′ x 13′ x 13′ cost $3999, the $999 representing overtime for the men who worked all night before departure-time. Transportation to Barcelona and Madrid was $9569. This included a motorcycle escort hired by the mayor of Madrid to escort the horse-drawn trailer with the crate through the narrow streets of the Spanish capital to the Cultural City. (D1955, April 1, 15, 25) Mazas, whom Archer had invited to represent him and Anna at the unveiling ceremony May 17, departed May 10. Archer gave him $5000 to cover expenses. Anna must have been pleased to have Archer pitch in to defray costs.

By early June Mazas returned and visited the Huntingtons so they could hear a tape he had made at the ceremony. Afterwards, wanting Archer's voice on his tape, he asked him to read a few poems and answer questions. The ailing Hispanophile cooperated until the last question. Then, irritated by Mazas' fuss and bustle, worn out with pain in his hips, he lay back in his wheelchair, saying with a wave of his large white hand, "Nada name. Nada name." ("No more. No more.") Noticing how crestfallen Mazas looked, Anna filled in. "When doing the symbolical *Torch Bearer* I had in mind the heroism of the Spanish people who had held for centuries to their ideals, and today in their University City can lead the world." (D1955, June 3)

1. Edwards. 65.

2. Cesare Contini, interview by George Gurney, for *Archives of American Art*, Smithsonian Institution, Washington, D.C. Microfilm 3612.

3. See Chapter 7.

4. Elisabeth Gordon Chandler to Mary Mitchell, 3 May 2003. Mrs. Chandler founded the Lyme Academy and guided and developed it into a College of Fine Arts, Old Lyme, Connecticut. It will bestow its first B.F.A. and M.F.A. in 2004. She teaches three courses in sculpture at the present time. While a young sculptor, Mrs. Chandler looked up to Anna Hyatt Huntington as her idol. She kindly volunteered to read this chapter on Anna's sculpture and critique it.

5. Ibid., 19 February 2003.

6. Records, Woodlawn Cemetery, Bronx, New York. The Huntington Mausoleum is located on Lots no. 30076, 3084, 7364, 7374. The plot is "Magnolia."

7. Chandler to Mary Mitchell, 5 February 2003. 3.

8. Harriet Mayer to AHH, 11 June 1952. *Incoming Letters*, General Correspondence, Series I, Box 5. AHH Papers.

9. Edwards. 67.

10. Ibid., 10.

11. Chandler to MM, 7 May 2003.

12. Quote from an unidentified poem by Matthew Arnold found in Roget's *International Thesaurus*, 1946. Thomas Y. Crowell Company. Section 70.1.

13. *Directory of American Scholars*, 7th ed. (v.3) 1978. R. R. Bowker & Co. 166.

CHAPTER 15

UNCLE ARCHER AND AUNT ANNA
1948

IT IS CHRISTMAS, 1948, in the living room at Stanerigg. Brantz Mayor trips the self-timer on his camera, then scampers around the tripod to perch beside his niece, Martha, smile, and be included in the picture. The photograph shows the immediate family of his Aunt Anna, the children and grandchildren of her sister, Harriet Hyatt Mayor. Harriet, Brantz's mother, sits to the left, and all the children are her grandchildren, Anna's great-nieces and great-nephews. Everyone seems to be enjoying the occasion except the host, Uncle Archer. He looks as if he is putting up with the happy confusion of ten young people excited by Christmas and arranging themselves to be photographed, a painful, boring ordeal he must endure in order to participate in the dinner all will soon enjoy. On that day the roads from New York City to Redding, Connecticut, are icy and treacherous, and Sherry, the caterer, has telephoned he will be late with the fixings.

Aunt Anna, on the other hand, sits erect and alert, her favorite people surrounding her. A month previous she had a cataract removed from her left eye, and now wears some new trifocals. On her head is her new white wig, marcelled and clean. She was glad to have it, for, as she wrote Harriet when the two wigs came, one to wear, one to wash, she would otherwise be "hairless, as well as eyeless and toothless." (D1948, August 8)

Anna's talents and accomplishments are abundant and spectacular and have often been written about. But never described is another side of her nature, equally compulsive, that became stronger the older she grew. She was a very domestic woman who loved housekeeping, and if in an interval when a change-over between maids left the pantry empty she welcomed the chance to do the dishes and clean up the pantry. She enjoyed people and particularly, entertaining her family. "Family," for Anna was not a gray and indifferent word. Resonating warmth, love and affection, faith and trust, it was a word full of nostalgia for her happy childhood on the family farm at Annisquam, or "Squam" as it was usually called.

At first, when she married Archer, she had not tried to bring her family into their life. But then observing him talk with her mother and laugh with her sister Harriet, about arthritic problems and remedies, she started inviting her family to visit. At Thanksgiving time Brookgreen Gardens always sent up express some fifteen turkeys and wild ducks the Huntingtons ordered every year. After settling in at

Edmund   Ridgeley   Maria Ann   Alfred   Harriet-V Virginia   Katheri

Harriet   Chu-Chu   Archer   Brantz   Anna   Martha   Susan - Michael,

Anna's extended family at Christmas Dinner 1948 at Stanerigg.

Stanerigg Archer suggested engaging Sherry's, a popular New York caterer, to take over the family luncheon. He had the chef come to Stanerigg, planned the menu and negotiated the cost. The war intervened, entertaining ceased, and then came the bimonthly trek to New York to deliver coins. But

after these interruptions, he said he would do all the ordering. Delighted, Anna encouraged him. As the children grew older and began to think ahead to college and a career, he was always ready to listen. Finding Uncle Archer so approachable and friendly, Hyatt and Brantz came often with their families,

132

bringing their friends, to swim, help walk the dogs, gather eggs in the chicken coop, and if a change of job was in the offing discuss it with Uncle Archer.

While writing this book we posted notices in regional libraries and town halls that we were seeking anecdotes, photos, and lore about the Huntingtons. By the slimmest of chances Sandra Cook, daughter of Ridgely Cook who was Harriet Mayor's grandson and Anna's great-nephew, saw our notice in the C. H. Booth Library in Newtown. She put us in touch with her Mayor cousins, several of whom kindly replied to our requests for reminiscences of Uncle Archer and Aunt Anna.

"Things were quite formal while Uncle Archer was living," wrote Ana, Brantz Mayor's wife. "Meals were served in the dining room by two maids in black and white uniforms. Spanish wine was always served with the meal over which Uncle Archer presided. We had access only to the social rooms and the studio. He had a great sense of humor, teased a lot, and was somewhat of a flirt, often spouting Arabic. He conversed with me in Spanish—I'm an Argentinian. He was very good to Aunt Anna. She said she had to be careful of what she said in front of him for he would dash out to get whatever she wished for.

"While Brantz joined Uncle Archer in his study to discuss world matters, Anna, depending on the seasons, would take us walking, swimming, sledding, or skating. When we swam it was usually by the old boat dock. We often swam to Rock Island in Hopewell Lake and picnicked there, then returned to tea. Visitors from New York or elsewhere would already be there. She had tea at 4 p.m. Saturday, Sunday, Monday and Tuesday for whomever was in the house. When we came as a family—Brantz and I had

Uncle Archer with his great-nephew, Archer Mayor, son of Brantz and Ana Mayor, ca. 1951.

7 children—we always slept in one of three cottages across Sunset Hill road. I recall we slept in one called Blueberry."[1]

One happy result of Archer's marrying into the numerous Hyatt-Mayor clan, took Anna by surprise. Harriet told Anna about a conversation her grand-

133

son, Ridgely Cook, had had with his father, Edmund Cook. After the divorce, the father agreed to pay for his sons' educations. But on May 18, 1947, he called Ridgely to tell him that he (old Edmund) was going to stop paying for his education as he wanted to build a house and could not afford to go on spending money on the boys. So Ridgely told his father that was all right by him. He needn't worry about it. Uncle Archer had given him money to get his education. "My father was flabbergasted," said Ridgely. (D1947, 18 May) This tells a lot about a millionaire who shunned publicity, never wrote or told anything about himself, and never told his wife what he was doing for her great-nephews.

A great-niece, Martha Mayor Smith, Hyatt Mayor's daughter, also remembers Archer and Anna from celebrating Christmas and Thanksgiving at Stanerigg and visiting between holidays. "They were very kind, affectionate, and generous to everyone. They loved seeing family and friends and made everyone feel completely welcome."[2]

In 1950 Anna staged two gala occasions. New Year's fell on Sunday. So that afternoon she and Archer welcomed seventy people to eggnog in the studio and champagne in the living room. Many children also came, so she had juices for them and gave each a lump of clay to fool with. Then on March 10, their 3-in-1-Day, "we had a great family party to toast Archer's 80th—18 all told. They brought a lot of amusing toys and cards to explain them. Hyatt wrote most of them. Archer had cables and telegrams and flowers galore." (D1950, March 10)

Since the family was so accustomed to being at Stanerigg for special occasions, it is no wonder Katherine, Anna's niece, chose the "concrete block monastery" as some had called Stanerigg, for her wedding to Blake Townsend, a second wedding for both of them, on August 9, 1949. "I moved furniture around on the patio," wrote Anna, "to make space for 6 small tables with 25 people expected. The ceremony was on the terrace against a background of the weeping beech. Archer gave the bride away. We put chairs on the terrace and in the covered part of the porch. The Rev. Houston came early, but the bridal couple did not get here until nearly 2 p.m., having been caught in a traffic jam in the city. Finally we had lunch and everyone seemed happy. Brantz took candid shots to his heart's delight and toasted the bride. The temp. was 92 degrees. Afterwards, the men went down to the lake to swim and cool off. They all departed about 5 after a really successful party." (D1949, August 9)

* * *

IN CALIFORNIA there lived another family clan that Anna gave presents to. A generation older than the children in the photograph, these people were the children and grandchildren of Archer's first cousin, Henry Edwards Huntington, the founder of The Huntington Library and Art Collections in San Marino, California. The relationship came about because Henry's father was Solon Huntington, and Archer's father was Collis, Solon's brother. Each of Henry's four children had children who in turn had their families.[3] Anna had never met any of them except Henry who was Arabella's second husband. But she knew they were a close-knit group, taking part in each other's weddings, traveling together and visiting back and forth. Accordingly, after the war when she had to confront the mass of linens, silver, china, tapestries and other household embellishments that had accumulated and been stored at No. 1 East Eighty-ninth Street, she immediately thought of Archer's relatives as logical recipients. She never wondered if they would want any of these things. She just assumed that because they were objects of such fine quality one couldn't find anywhere today, that of course they would be glad to receive them. Anna was a thrifty New Englander, and getting rid of possessions by giving to a thrift shop, holding a tag sale, or calling the Salvation Army never occurred to her.

She started "clearing out" in March of 1946 while down at Atalaya. Annie worked with her to sort "all the things that have been left over while we have been down here." As they worked, they reminisced how Anna and Archer had outfitted guest-cottages, housed servants colored and white, and had 25 beds to take care of at one time. (D1946, February 19) Putting away only the "bare necessities," they packed up a huge pile to ship to No. 1 in New York. (D1946, March 29)

A month later, she and Annie were again sorting, this time in New York on the fifth floor of No. 1, surrounded by cases and crates of pewter, china and glass, linens of all kinds, towels, sheets, blanket-covers, even a silver tea-set. Shocked to see "such a raft of stuff that had accumulated in storage for years," Anna said, "Now is the time to give to family. One can't buy any linen at all today. Such lovely stuff that is no longer made either here or abroad. Have spent all my married life trying to get rid of things." (D1946, April 17, 22; May 1)

The "lovely stuff" came from several sources. There was a pile from "The Homestead," a country house at Throgg's Neck in Westchester where Collis and Arabella had lived until he died in 1900 and which Arabella retained to pass on to Archer. Then there were linens from 1083 Fifth Avenue where Archer and his first wife, Helen, had lived for twenty-three years; linens from Rocas, the mansion at Haverstraw, New York, which Archer had bought furnished from Sam Katz, the movie mogul; linens from Camp Arbutus, the rustic camp in the Adirondacks that Archer had given to Syracuse University in 1934. And more abundant than from anywhere else, linens from No. 2 East Fifty-seventh Street, New York, which Anna had cleared out in 1926 before it was demolished and where Arabella had lived for thirty-five years. Sixty pairs of yellow silk lace curtains for that monstrous house of five floors and sixty rooms, were a big part of the pile from Arabella's palace.

Still another heap massive enough to fill eight van-loads when it was shipped to the States, came from the Chateau Beauregard at Versailles near Paris which Henry and Arabella had leased in 1914 after their marriage in 1913. Residing in a romantic French Chateau was a whim of Arabella's. The number of rooms in the Chateau is unknown, but its size can be estimated by the fact that the staff recruited and hired was thirteen for the inside and nineteen for the outside.[4] She adored redecorating and refurnishing any large residence and did a total job. When World War I was over, after two years of living there, she hated to give in to Henry's more practical outlook and pack up. Everything but one big item was to be shipped to the west coast. This was a medieval tapestry of a hunting scene, long and colorful, that Anna set aside. "I'll hang this on my studio wall at Stanerigg," she said as she and Annie hauled the heavy thing to one side. (D1946, April 22)

The general destination for these "linens" was San Francisco and Los Angeles where Henry Edwards Huntington had lived most of his life. When Anna was finished, eight van-loads and nineteen trunks, and uncounted numbers of cases, barrels, and crates were shipped to Southern California. Annie then announced she was retiring to her native Newfoundland after twenty years working for the Huntingtons. "So from now on," said Anna, "arranging all these things will be my job." (D1950, November 17)

1. Ana Mayor to AG, 22 October 2002: 22 April, 6 May, 3 June 2003.

2. Martha Mayor Smith to AG, 4 April 2003.

3. Thorpe. 165–176.

4. Ibid., 336.

CHAPTER 16

"MY DEAREST ARCHER"

1955

THE STORY of Archer's final year should start with July instead of January, for during the first part of the year he was almost his normal self, feisty, generous, decisive, empathetic. He paid hospital bills for a close friend, and bought a sculpture, *St. George and the Dragon*, from another who was trying to establish herself in the artistic community. When his heartbeat became irregular and Anna called in a pathologist, Archer scorned the prescribed drug, because the doctor couldn't tell him what was in it.

Occasionally he put on his executive hat. Dr. West, president of the Numismatic Society, told him riff-raff and delinquents were getting into Audubon Terrace at night, and he wanted to fence off access to it at the Broadway entrance. The watchman couldn't handle the situation. Archer directed him to go ahead and do it. He'd pay for the fence. Then in September, on learning that both the American Indian Museum and the Geographical Society, the two institutions on Audubon Terrace closest to Broadway on the east, strenuously objected to any fence, Archer ordered the fence pushed back to protect only the Hispanic Society and the Numismatic Society. (D1955, May 7; September 26)

Archer knew that his health was on an irreversible

slide. Two years ago, he had told his friend, the Cuban journalist José García-Mazas, that he knew he had only two more years to live. Talking more freely in Spanish to his Cuban friend than he did to Anna, he described his "economic philosophy." He said it "consisted in believing himself an 'administrator' of the fortune left to him by his father, but not the 'owner.' That is why before his death and far in advance of it," wrote Mazas, "he left many of his properties to cultural institutions as, for example, the University of Syracuse (N.Y.) to which he left the vast parcels of land in the Adirondack mountains that contained primary forests and lakes with flora and fauna; Brookgreen Gardens to the State of South Carolina; the Mariners' Museum to the State of Virginia; and after his wife's death the land except for Stanerigg to the State of Connecticut to be converted into a state park. A few days before he died he said to me, 'My mission has been accomplished.'"[1]

Most of the time Anna walked a tightrope. When the doctor prescribed a new drug to make him sleep, she had to cajole him into trying one pill and hope the result would encourage him to continue. He did and had a good night's sleep, the first in many weeks. She never fussed or hovered, but stayed near. With

137

two exceptions Anna did not leave Stanerigg for eleven months. The pistol Archer had always kept within reach had become rusty, and he worried, unable to sleep. The next day Anna went in to Danbury and bought him one. (D1955, May 4) On the second occasion, when she discovered he was carrying a copy of his will in his pajama pocket, she said that was a dangerous practice, and drove into town to buy him a small safe where he could keep the document at hand by his bed. (D1955, June 24)

Her attentions for his comfort were unflagging. Screening everyone who called to visit, she would consider the request and if she thought it necessary, turn the person away. "It used to hurt to say no," she said. "But bores have hardened me." (D1955, April 23) Used to daily exercise while walking dogs around Hopewell Lake, she found it hard not to urge Archer to try strolling about the farmyard. Even though he knew his legs were wobbly and couldn't support him when dressing himself, he didn't want to walk. Exercise bored him. (D1955, August 8) He'd get along somehow. Anna had stopped urging him, and instead, helped him to dress.

Harboring doubts, she nevertheless discussed with Archer having a few people for tea on a Sunday in May. Archer agreed. He would try it. Friends and family came. For an hour he sat in his wheelchair at a small table by the dining room and served all who came with a slice of chocolate home-baked cake. Leesome, a big grey deerhound, stood at his side, anticipating, never snatching, the slice he was always given. Mazas was there with his recorder. Bucked up by the general cheerful mood, the aging Hispanophile forgot his troubles and recited a poem from the Koran. But the exertion was too much.

Growing hoarse, he had himself wheeled into his study, staying until all was quiet. (D1955, September 25)

Watching Archer quote from the Koran, Anna remembered him as he was seven years before, when she had her first cataract operation in November 1948. "He came twice a day to see me for two hours in the morning and 3:15 to 4 pm in the afternoon. My nurse says the nurses are all a-twitter over how he removes his hat when entering the elevator and steps aside to let them precede him out the door. They ask if he was the handsome, very tall man dressed in grey with a chauffeur who helped him in and out of the limousine. They pronounced him a gentleman." (D1948, November 12)

This image crowded her mind as she wheeled him out of his room to welcome "the girls" from the Hispanic Society. Around the first of August they came but did not visit with him. Archer must have agreed to this procedure, for throughout, he sat in his wheelchair in the hall near his study and watched. They spent three hours sorting out books from his personal library, packing them in crates, and transferring them to a truck which would then transport them to the Hispanic Society in New York. This upset him. Pounding his fist on the arm of the chair, he grew angry and said he thought they were going directly to the Society. Hastily removing some books from the truck and stacking them in her car, one of them, Miss Johnson, drove away. Pacified, Archer slumped in his chair and was wheeled into his room. Eventually, over the following weeks, 42 boxes and 20 crates of Spanish, Arabic, and French volumes, totaling some 500 books, and their bookcases, were removed and transported to New York. More than any other development, this indicated his resignation as to the future. (D1955, August 2; September 1, 6, 9, 29, 30)

Soon other disturbing symptoms occurred. His bed had been moved down to his study, and a cot for Anna wedged in there too. A hospital bed replaced his old familiar bed. Bewildered, he called Anna a dozen times a night to know where he was. (D1955, October 1) Dizzy from four successive falls, he attacked her as she tried to keep him from getting out of bed. Fortunately, nothing was broken in these falls.

During odd moments when he was asleep or in a coma, Anna wrote Christmas cards, packed, sorted, and arranged linens to send to the west coast, and directed Contini who came to clear out her studio. She sorted files in Miss Perkins's office. A single critical hurdle had to be crossed. The lawyer, Wendell Davis, whom Archer trusted, presented him to sign a Power of Attorney, which as yet he had never given Anna. The bills were mounting and she needed cash. Seeing his wild, scrawling signature on other papers, Anna and Davis helped Archer make his mark on the signature line to validate it. (D1955, October 10)

In November, a pleasant event brought a reprieve. Brookgreen Gardens asked Archer to ship down to be sold any books of his poetry he had kept back. Immediately, the spirits of this longtime poet, whose first of six books of poetry had been published in 1936, revived. He crawled out of his bed, worked his way to a cupboard, holding onto the moldings of the wall, and got out thirty books to send to Brookgreen. Within two weeks, all had been sold to visitors. (D1955, September 21; November 16) Rejuvenated, Archer made a legible signature on documents from

the Bank of New York and the Central Hanover Bank.

During the last week he grew confused, would not eat, and fought the doctor who tried in vain to inject a sedative in his veins. Five days before the end, Mazas visited "the unparalleled Hispanist" and wrote, "That millionaire did not wear on his hands even the adornment of a gold ring. Even the watch he wore at the moment of his death was not worth more than thirty dollars. (He gave me his own gold watch.) Some of his pajamas had as many patches on them as those of a common European clerk . . . He felt weak, in pain, losing his sight, and those hallucinations that he suffered in the afternoons made him fear for his mental faculties . . . He was in bed in a mended blue pajama. The large bony hands, so powerful in other times now remained still on the white blanket. A light shone in his opaque eyes as he looked at me. He smiled. He squeezed my hand and then lifted himself up in that humble iron bed. With a hollow and weak voice he once again sang to me the Aragonese *jota* that Leopoldo, his mountain guide in the Pyrenees, had taught him,

Anoche te vi la cara,
A la luz de mi cigarro-o-o . . . [2]

Then he dropped back saying he could do no more."

"At the end," wrote Anna on that Sunday evening, "he tried to get out of bed. I called the doctor to inject more sedative. He looked badly. But to no avail. Sunday, December 11, at 3 a.m., while he slept, my dearest Archer peacefully died." (D1955, December 11)

Three days later, came the funeral at the Church of Heavenly Rest situated next to 1083 Fifth Avenue in New York. "In the church the flowers were a mass of color. We had to increase cars as all from Stanerigg wanted to come. 18 from the Hispanic Society, tears running down the cheeks of all the girls. Contini, Mr. and Mrs. Mazas, the Spanish Consul, the president of the National Sculpture Society.

"After the funeral and the cemetery, Brantz, Ana, and their four children, Harriet, Hyatt and Virginia, Katherine and Blake all stayed with me and slept well.[3] It was lovely to have my family all under one roof and hope it will happen often."

Archer left Anna his own kind of solace. The poem appeared in his last book of poetry called *The Torch Bearer*, published in 1954 and dedicated to her.

> To you whose joyous smile across the haze
> Of weariness, could flood with light the days,
> And fold the valley of our journeying,
> Even in the silvery dawn of spring.
> To you my heart, as might a sunlit sea,
> Welcome your soul, ship of my destiny!
> With you in splendor past all dreams' desire,
> I found a world lighted by love's true fire.

1. G-M, *El Poeta*. 485ff.
2. Ibid. 489f. Spanish verse translated: "Last night I saw your face By the light of my cigarette."

3. AMH was interred in the Collis P. Huntington Mausoleum, Woodlawn Cemetery, Bronx, New York.

POSTSCRIPT

The postscript tells what happened in Anna's remaining years. Since the emphasis in this book is on Anna and Archer's marriage, we read her diaries only through the year Archer died. For this last section, however, we have relied on other sources including descendants of Anna's extended family. She continued sculpting for seventeen more years. Susan Edwards records that in this last period Anna produced seventy-two dated pieces of sculpture out of a lifetime total of approximately five hundred.[1] Never since Anna and Archer were married could she indulge her craft so freely nor need it so much to dispel her loneliness. Money matters did not worry her, for Archer had left her with a life income derived from $7,000,000 in trusts. This was in addition to her income from annuities he had given her at various times after they moved to Connecticut. So now we will tell about her sculpture, her family, the fate of Stanerigg, and about their wills.

After Archer died Anna's sister, Harriet Hyatt Mayor, moved from Princeton, New Jersey, to Stanerigg to live until she died in December 1960. The family came often to visit. "Anna and Harriet were always laughing and joking together," recalls Sandra Cook, Harriet's great-granddaughter. "We called them the 'dynamic duo.' And they were also good rifle shots. Anna loved her birdfeeder which also attracted squirrels. I remember her getting 15 squirrels in no time at all."

Sandra described the house as she remembered it. "Books were everywhere. Many pictures, paintings and decorations were on the concrete walls. On the walls of the large hall were many hunting trophies. The children thought Uncle Archer caught them. He was an avid fisherman, but apparently did not hunt, and purchased all the trophies in the Huntington Lodge trophy room at Camp Arbutus in the Adirondacks. We often walked counterclockwise around Hopewell Lake with Anna and several deerhounds. She stopped breeding pups, and gradually, the number of deerhounds diminished, although there were still a few older ones around when Aunt Harriet was there. After Uncle Archer died we could roam the house, the maids were gone, and we ate in the livingroom or outdoors."[2]

For two months after Archer's death, Anna did not enter her studio. But on February 23, 1956, she finished a memorial for her husband and herself. This was *The Visionaries*, an idealized concept of Anna and Archer planning Brookgreen Gardens and other wildlife sanctuaries. He had seen it before he died and liked the idea, although she felt it a little odd to create a statue of herself and Archer—but who better?[3] She liked to place every piece of sculpture accepted by Brookgreen. Her choice for *The Visionaries* was the middle of a reflecting pool.

Once again in her studio, Anna entered a period of almost constant creative activity. Encouraged by José

The Visionaries by Anna Hyatt Huntington. 1955 Brook-green Gardens. Anna and Archer planning the gardens.

García-Mazas, she had presented a replica of the Madrid *Torch Bearer* group to Cuba. This led to Anna's being asked to create a piece more specifically Cuban. She replied she would do her best, God willing, as she was eighty years old, but hoped to be spared long enough to deserve the confidence placed in her.[4]

For a subject she chose an equestrian statue of José Martí (1853–1895), a patriot who fought for Cuba's freedom from Spanish rule. Considered the Cuban equivalent of George Washington, many Cuban villages have either a statue of him, or a street named after him. Anna chose to depict the moment Martí and his horse were mortally wounded in ambush when hit by Spanish bullets on May 19, 1895.[5] She completed the statue in 1956, but it was not installed at the corner of 59th and Sixth Avenue

by Central Park in New York City until 1965. This was because the United States Department of State feared repercussions. Cuba was free, but Fidel Castro was in power.[6] Cubans in New York City raised $100,000 for the pedestal. Anna gave the statue to New York.

During a lull in her creative work, Anna, accompanied by the faithful Miss Perkins, visited Brook-green Gardens to confer with the trustees there. Then they drove to Mariners' Museum at Newport News to visit with the staff and director.

The next day they went to Huntington, West Virginia, a city founded by Collis P. Huntington in 1871 when he was developing the Chesapeake & Ohio railroad network in the southeast. They wanted to see the bronze statue of Collis standing in front of the C&O depot. Arabella Huntington had commissioned Gutzon Borglum to do it. It was unveiled just six weeks after Arabella's death in 1924.[7]

After these breaks Anna was again busy in her studio producing a string of pieces inspired by incidents in American history. First, there was a dramatic bronze statue 12′ high of Sybil Ludington, a teenage Paul Revere. Sixteen years old in 1777, the eldest of twelve children, Sybil was putting the younger children to bed on the night of April 26, 1777, when word reached her home that the British were burning the town of Danbury, Connecticut, twenty-five miles away. Her father was a colonel in the local militia which was scattered over a wide area around the Ludington house in Carmel, New York. Sybil convinced her father to let her ride out on her horse and summon the men. Riding sidesaddle over forty miles on dark, unmarked roads, through Carmel, Mahopac and what is now Ludingtonville, the courageous girl spread the alert. The men gathered in time to rout the British and send them back to their ships in Long Island Sound. Anna's statue of this intrepid young woman on her bronze steed stands on the western shore of Lake Gleneida in Carmel, New York.

Abraham Lincoln as a subject did not occur to Anna until she found out he rode a horse for his job.[8] Twenty-two years old, he left his family in Springfield, Illinois, to settle in New Salem, a raw pioneer town twenty-five miles north on the Sangamon River. Here he became postmaster in 1833 and stuffed the mail in his hat as he rode about the town to deliver it.[9] Anna's first statue of *Young Abe Lincoln on a Horse* went to New Salem, Illinois, in 1961.

The second statue was placed on the Illinois Pavilion at the World's Fair in the summer of 1964. On February 3, 1965, the 7,500-pound statue joined the Atlantic Fleet Amphibious force by boarding the attack transport USS *Mountrail* at Norfolk, Virginia, for a trip whose ultimate destination was Salzburg, Austria. The statue was a gift from the sculptor and the National Arts Foundation president, Dr. Carlton Smith. Salzburg was chosen as the permanent site of the statue because it served as the site of the American Occupational Headquarters in Austria after World War II. The donation of the statue was the result of a visit to New Salem, Illinois, by Dr. Heinrich Drimmel, the former Austrian Minister of Education and a Lincoln enthusiast.

It was dedicated April 14, 1965, the 10th anniversary of Austria's freedom from Germany and the 100th anniversary of the assassination of President Abraham Lincoln. In addition to the one in New Salem, Illinois, there are four other *Young Abe Lincolns*, in Hoboken, New Jersey, Lincoln City, Ore-

Harriet moved up to Stanerigg from Princeton, New Jersey, and lived with Anna until she died in 1960.

gon, Redding, Connecticut, and Syracuse University, New York.[10]

In the next few years Anna did a number of smaller pieces. A prominent one was *The Opening of the West*, 1964, an 8-foot high bronze of Collis P. Huntington, seated with a map on his lap as he peered westward over the James River by the Newport News Shipyard in Newport News, Virginia. A plaque on the brick pedestal bears the inscription, "We shall build good ships here at a profit if we can, at a loss if we must, but always good ships."

A year later she produced another historic horseman, *The Young Jackson*. As a young man of seventeen, the seventh president of the United States is seated bareback on a farm horse in the Andrew Jackson Historical State Park, Lancaster, South Carolina.

Eighty-one years old now, she next tackled one of her more unusual subjects. She had been corresponding with a fighter squadron commander at the

Myrtle Beach Air Force Base, who wanted an emblem for his unit. Her suggestion of "a spirited fighting panther" was accepted, and she started work on August 7, 1957. The piece was ready for casting on September 21.[11]

A common remark about Anna's sculpture has to do with the material she used. Anna was the first sculptor to use aluminum. Cerinda Evans once asked her why she chose aluminum. Anna replied that she liked its vibrant quality; it was more filled with light than bronze. In the last four years she had chosen aluminum for the cast of twenty or more figures sent to as many museums from Rockland, Maine, to Racine, Wisconsin.[12]

Her last statue was that of General Israel Putnam, an American Revolutionary general, who, with fist raised and shouting defiance, in 1778 urged his nervous steed down a flight of steps in Greenwich, Connecticut, to escape the pursuing British. Henry Rasmussen told us that Anna completed the statue with no destination in mind. When the Connecticut Department of Transportation declined her offer to install it at the Connecticut welcoming center on Interstate 84 near the New York border, she asked Henry if he had a place to suggest. He suggested the Putnam Memorial State Park just two miles from Stanerigg.

The day of the dedication Mrs. Rasmussen, Anna's dressmaker, made sure Anna's dress and hat looked right. Anna left in her limousine. Mrs. Rasmussen left separately. At the hour-long dedication September 21, 1969, Mrs. Rasmussen was dismayed to see Anna in her tennis shoes. Anna explained, "They were comfortable." Anna stood through the hour-long ceremony. The *General* was appropriately

General Israel Putnam escaping from the British at Greenwich, Connecticut, 1778. Anna's last piece, done when she was 91 years old. Credit, A. S. Goodrich.

placed at the entrance to the site of his 1778–1779 encampment in Redding, near a lake in Putnam Memorial State Park.

Henry Rasmussen helped Anna in other ways. He supervised the outside crew at Stanerigg when, after Archer's death, Anna had a total staff of sixteen working at the farm and around the estate.[13]

As Doris Cook, her dedicated biographer, wrote in 1976, "The Putnam statue that was completed when Anna was ninety-one and unveiled when she was ninety-three, was the final big challenge Anna would welcome. Illness forced her to give up going

Young Abe Lincoln on a Horse, left to Syracuse University after Anna's death. Credit, A. S. Goodrich.

to her studio in 1972. On October 4, 1973, the wondrous shaping hands of Anna Hyatt Huntington lay still."[14]

On October 7 a memorial service was held at St. Thomas Episcopal Church in Bethel after which she was interred with her "dearest Archer" in the Collis P. Huntington mausoleum at Woodlawn Cemetery in the Bronx, New York City.

Memory of Anna Huntington remains vivid for many people. David Gesualdi, sculptor, teacher of sculpture, and owner of the prototype Nebel enlarging machine, recalled that when he was thirteen in

1972 he visited Anna with his father, Anna's eye doctor. He confided to her that he wanted to be a sculptor. "She had recently had a stroke, and at that point wasn't able to speak, but she fixed me with a look that I can't quite explain. She somehow conveyed in that one look the importance that sculpture had in her life. It changed the way I looked at sculpture forever."[15]

Even Yeardley Smith, Anna's great-grandnephew, age six at the time, recalls that "Aunt Anna, though very old and not completely mobile, was always up for a pillow fight with soft sofa pillows. I used to go to her studio and wonder what she saw in those big lumps of clay. I now have three of her sculptures which I love, two bears playing, a mother giraffe with her baby, and a mother elephant helping her baby out of the mud. I remember Anna as being very proper and elegant, but warm, kind, and approachable."[16]

The *Wolf Group* and the *Bear Group*, which Anna finished in 1954, were placed on their stone pedestals at the main entrance to the park on Sunset Hill Road in Redding.

After her death the Stanerigg mansion was demolished. Henry Rasmussen recalls the demolition contractor had a difficult time tearing down the roof. The ceiling beams were sheathed with ¼-inch copper to ensure it was fireproof. The contractor made a tremendous profit from selling the copper.[17]

Another major event that Archer had arranged for in 1950 happened after Anna died. The state of Connecticut received 694 acres of Stanerigg for the Collis P. Huntington State Park. In 1985 the remainder of the property was sold to Mr. and Mrs. John Angeloni who established a horseback riding school.

According to Anna, Archer was often the life of the party. But in all our searches we found no evidence of that. Then one day at the Syracuse Library this picture of a smiling Archer slid out of a batch of family photographs. A smile to remember at the end of our Chronicle.

Anna, caught in a rare moment of inactivity, hands caressing her devoted dogs. A widow now, she may be brooding on the past. But this widow has never dwelt in the past, only in the present and the immediate future. She is planning where to place *The Visionaries*, a sculpture she started before Archer died and has just finished. It shows a young man and woman planning Brookgreen Gardens. (Photographer unknown)

The large garage became a stable; the kennels were converted into apartments, and the greenhouse area became a riding ring.

Archer signed his will February 21, 1941, in Hartford, Connecticut, and left no codicils. The value of his estate at death was set at $3,364,000, which included cash of $1,594,000 in eleven bank accounts, securities and accumulated income thereon of $1,552,000, and accumulated income of $165,000 on twenty-two life income trusts. He had established these trusts amounting to some $7,900,000 between 1930 and 1953. Eighteen of them amounting to $7,500,000 went to Anna for life income, then on her death were distributed among the Huntington Free Library, Hispanic Society of America, Heye Foundation, California Palace of Legion of Honor,

Mariners' Museum, Brookgreen Museum, American Academy of Arts and Letters, and Southwest Texas State Teachers College.[18]

In summing up Archer's philanthropic activity for his *History of Redding, Connecticut*, Frank W. Nye wrote that in Archer's lifetime he gave away $50,000,000, or approximately $330,000,000 in today's money.[19] Nye was writing in 1956 before the Huntingtons' Papers were open to the public. An exceedingly generous man, Archer Huntington shunned publicity, and gave away much more than was ever publicly recorded. We will never exactly know how many millions he did give away.

Archer had also transferred ownership of Camp Arbutus to Syracuse University; and Camp Pine Knot, inherited from his father, went to the State University of New York. (See appendices for their stories.)

Anna's estate was fixed at $3,373,000, comprised of $800,000 in real estate, $1,667,000 in stocks and bonds, $718,000 in cash, $113,000 accrued under the twenty-two trusts, and $43,000 miscellaneous. Of her personal belongings, she left to the Hispanic Society a drawing of Archer by Jean de Avalos, and to her nephew, Brantz Mayor, a marble bust of herself by Harriet.

To Syracuse University she left all personal records of a biographical nature, portraits of Archer, Archer's mother, Arabella, and his father, Collis, a death mask of Collis, and portraits of Anna's mother, Audella Beebe Hyatt, her sister Harriet Mayor, and her brother Alpheus Hyatt.

To Syracuse she also left the bronze and aluminum statuary of her own design, which were in the course of fabrication at the time of her death. She authorized her executors to pay for completing all unfinished fabrications and to pay for shipment to the beneficiary.[20]

Thomas L. Cheney, the attorney who settled both Archer's and Anna's estates, recalls, "One piece not shipped to its beneficiary, Syracuse University, was *Young Abe Lincoln on a Horse*. It stood 13′ 9″ high on its pedestal and weighed about 7,500 pounds. I got a trucker to mount it on a truck in a tilted position to minimize its height, determine the height of the load, then find a route to Syracuse University where *Abe* wouldn't hit wires or bridges."[21] The trucker must have made a successful trip, for today, *Young Abe Lincoln on his Horse* stands alone and open to all weathers in the center of a grassy plot between Bray Hall and Walters Hall. Bray Hall is the administration building of the SUNY College of Environmental Science and Forestry (ESF) on the Syracuse University campus.

1. Edwards. 100–126.

2. Sandra Cook, interviewed by AG, 17 March 2003.

3. Doris E. Cook. 15.

4. Ibid.

5. Ibid., 15–18.

6. Fidel Castro became Prime Minister of Cuba January 1959.

7. Joseph Platania. "Collis P. Huntington: The Story behind the Monument and the Man." *Huntington Quarterly.* Summer/Autumn 1995. Huntington, West Virginia. 60–65.

8. William Longgood. "A Lifetime Spent in Molding Truth." *New York World-Telegram*, 27 April 1965.

9. William E. Gienapp. *Abraham Lincoln and Civil War America.* Oxford University Press, 2002. 18.

10. Cerinda W. Evans. *Anna Hyatt Huntington.* The Mariners' Museum. Newport News, Virginia, 1965. 47.

11. Cook, 15.

12. Evans, 42.

13. Henry Rasmussen, interview by Albert Goodrich, Spring 2000.

14. Cook, 15.

15. David Gesualdi. "Enlarging Machine." *National Sculpture Society News Bulletin.* August/September 2000. 7.

16. Yeardley Smith to AG, 12 April 2003.

17. Henry Rasmussen, interviewed by AG, Spring 2002.

18. Will and Estate Inventory, Archer M. Huntington. Probate Records, Redding, Connecticut. V.24. 359–360.

19. Frank W. Nye. "Famous People." *History of Redding, Connecticut. Redding Times*, November 8, 1956. The Mark Twain Library in Redding does not have this book as such. A reference librarian gave us a printout of articles from the book on the Internet.

The equivalent of $50,000,000 in 1955 is approximately $330,000,000 in today's money. The conversion factor for 1955 is 6.6605. The source for this information is a table entitled "Purchasing Power Conversion Factors" found in *Research Reports*, Vol. LXIX No. 1. January 14, 2002. American Institute of Economic Research, Great Barrington, Massachusetts. 4.

20. Will of Anna Hyatt Huntington. Probate Records, Redding, Connecticut. V. 39. 840–850.

21. Thomas L. Cheney, telephone interview with AG, Summer 2002.

PINE KNOT

COLLIS P. HUNTINGTON and Thomas Durant first met and in the 1860s when they were bitter rivals. Collis was forging the Central Pacific Railroad eastward and Thomas was forging the Union Pacific Railroad westward in a fierce struggle to lay as much track as they could before eventually meeting at Promontory Point in Utah in 1869. Their railroads were paid according to the miles of track each laid.[1]

In 1876 Thomas's son William West Durant first visited the Adirondacks and in 1877 he built Camp Pine Knot, first of the famous Great Camps of the Adirondacks at Pine Knot Point on Raquette Lake. He sought to achieve an atmosphere of intimacy with nature. Birch bark covered the interior walls. Cedar was employed for furniture and massive porches with rustic railings. Twigs and branches were used for decorative rustic work. The woodland camps which Durant built included Camp Uncas, Sagamore, and Killcare.[2]

In 1882 he added the "Swiss Chalet" to Pine Knot. In 1885 his father died. Ten years later he sold Pine Knot with its 200 acres to Collis P. Huntington. In 1900 Collis died and Pine Knot passed to his wife Arabella.[3]

The family never returned to Pine Knot. Archer bought another of Durant's camps, Camp Arbutus, twenty-five miles to the east in Newcomb, New York, in 1900. His mother died in 1924 and Pine Knot passed to him. As hard as he tried Archer was unable to sell or give Pine Knot away.[4]

Finally Harlan Metcalf and Walter Thurber, faculty members of Cortland State College, 125 miles to the southwest, discovered it on a canoe trip to Raquette Lake in 1947.[5]

Harlan contacted Archer at his residence in Redding, Connecticut.

On January 15, 1948, Anna wrote in her diary, "President Smith of Teachers State College in upper New York came to see A- about transferring Pine Knot to that college as a place of outdoor education for their students and to be a memorial to CPH—to have his bust and a poem to him by A- on a plaque. Smith seemed much pleased to have the place and was going up to Albany to get the necessary papers and permit, etc. We are much pleased to get the place off our hands. It's been eating its head off since 1900—forty seven years."

In 1948 Governor Thomas E. Dewey signed a legislative act approving New York State acceptance of the facility.[6]

The main objectives of the Outdoor Education Centers programs are: to develop in all participants an attitude of appreciation for natural resources; to provide them with the knowledge to make informed environmental decisions; and to foster an understanding of ecological relationships, environmental concerns and human needs. It serves approximately 2,000 students a year.[7]

The name of Pine Knot was changed to Huntington Memorial Camp.

1. Ambrose, Stephen. *Nothing Like It in the World.* New York and London: Simon and Schuster. 2000.

2. Pamphlet *SUNY Cortland Outdoor Education Centers* at Raquette Lake. Cortland, New York. n.d.; no page numbers.

3. Ibid.

4. Ibid.

5. Ibid.

6. Ibid.

7. Ibid.

CAMP ARBUTUS

IN 1901 ARCHER bought Camp Arbutus from William West Durant, the originator of the Adirondack Great Camps. It was about 25 miles to the east of Pine Knot near Newcomb, New York. Eventually he acquired about 15,000 acres of surrounding land including Mt. Goodnow and several lakes.

By 1939 there was a cluster of fourteen buildings including the main residence, a combined dining-kitchen and servants unit, a guest house, studio, library and museum, a kennel, deer barn, generating plant, boat house, wood shed, servants quarters, laundry, and saw shed.[1] The studio was lined with white birch bark adorned with stuffed deer heads.

Anna kept deer of exotic species in a large fenced area attached to the studio. George Shaughnessy of Newcomb, who worked for the Huntingtons in the 1920s, remembers working with a horse trying to get it to lower its head so Mrs. Huntington could get a good photograph of the horse's neck muscles. George was using a handful of hay to entice the horse to lower its head when the horse bit through the hay and chomped on George's hand. He wasn't seriously injured but he was impressed with Mrs. Huntington's concern over his hand. He liked Mrs. Huntington, who he remembered as having a nice personality, someone easy to talk to. Archer, on the other hand, Mr. Shaughnessy remembers as cold and unfriendly, even provocative at times.[2]

Another of Mr. Shaughnessy's duties was to drive Anna's sculptures back and forth from Camp Arbutus to the New York City house. The house impressed him as being as big as a city block and had bars on the windows. One time he drove an unhappy eagle to the Bronx Zoo for Anna.[3]

The Huntingtons spent July and August at the camp during 1932–1935 but not in 1936–1938. Anna was feeling ill and summoned the Newcomb physician Dr. Johnson. He believed Mrs. Huntington had acquired tuberculosis based on what he heard in her chest. Because of Anna's importance he did not give her a saliva exam nor tell her his theory but used the State laboratory for the test. As it turned out Anna did have TB and was sick for nearly six years. Sometimes she was seen in a wheelchair at the camp. The camp was in an area well-known to be effective in curing some people of TB.[4]

One year they spent the whole winter at the camp. George Shaughnessy remembered cutting a tremendous amount of firewood. The woodshed held 500 cords of wood.[5]

One day Archer, an ardent fisherman, observed speckled trout in one of his brooks and got the idea their habitat might be improved. He hired a well-known surveyor to study the situation and was delighted his theory was correct. He hired a large crew of men to work in the winter to remove brush and rotted wood, and also build a road and ten dams. The result was ten most beautiful lakes. Archer had shown a way by which the Adirondacks may be clothed here and there with beautiful artificial lakes, enhancing their beauty and giving unlimited fishing grounds.[6]

The Huntingtons had two types of guide boats on the property—stationary boats that would stay on the major lakes and smaller, lighter boats to carry around to the minor waters. One day Tom Collard, a local person employed by the Huntingtons, was carrying a boat when Anna noticed it was a stationary boat, one she thought was too heavy for him. Since Archer was a big man and Anna didn't want her help abused, she made Archer carry the boat the rest of the way.[7]

Huntington hired a Spanish artist (probably Joaquin Sorolla y Bastida) to paint winter scenes of the view from Mt. Goodnow Mountain. These paintings were to be enlarged and hung in the library of Huntington's New York City residence.[8]

Since the Huntingtons had no children it might have been logical to suppose they might donate their Newcomb property to Cornell, which had a mile square forestry facility contiguous to the Huntington lands there: Archer had also funded Cornell student trips to South Carolina. But this was not the case—the property went to Syracuse University for the Forestry School.

One reason they gave the 13,000 acres to Syracuse University in 1932 may have been the result of a published account by Dean Leebrick of Syracuse. In it he praised the work of Anna Huntington's equestrian statue of Spain's medieval hero, El Cid Campeador. Archer, not easily moved by such methods, was pleased by the Dean's praise and soon after offered the property to Syracuse University. It should also be noted that Anna was awarded an honorary doctorate from Syracuse University in 1932. The apparent donation of 13,000 acres to the Forestry School followed shortly thereafter.[9]

The Huntingtons kept 2,000 acres along with Camp Arbutus. In 1939 they gave all of the remaining property to the Forestry School. The gifts were actually made to Syracuse University which lent it to the Forestry School, now called the State University of New York College of Environmental Science and Forestry, because of the Forever Wilds Law passed in 1894 which precludes the State from using forests for demonstration.

And what happened to Camp Arbutus?

It became the most important component of the research facilities of the Adirondack Ecological Center (AEC). The AEC was built in 1970 and dedicated in 1971. It became the focus of a more comprehensive program of understanding the Adirondack ecosystem through research. This Huntington 15,000 acres is surrounded by the 1.5 million-acre Adirondack Park providing abundant opportunities for ecological research.

There is housing for thirty people, conference room for fifty, a laboratory, shop space, computers, printers, specialized vehicles, the Adirondack Park Interpretive Center and an experienced technical staff. The research library was significantly expanded and has grown over the years with the support of the College of Environmental Science and Forestry's Moon Library at Syracuse University. It has over 2,500 volumes. In 1968 a series of lectures called the Huntington Lectures was started and still continues in what is called Huntington Lodge.[10]

1. Masters, Raymond D. *A Social History of The Huntington Wildlife Forest*. North Country Books, Inc. Utica, New York, 1993. Map page 96.

2. Ibid., 57.

3. Ibid., 58.

4. Ibid., 58.

5. Ibid., 60.

6. Ibid., 60.

7. Ibid., 61. See ref. to C. A. Bissell,1905. The Arbutus Lake Park Trout Water. *Forest and Stream*. 8 July 1905, 63:33.

8. Ibid., 61

9. Ibid., 64.

10. Ibid., 83.

ARCHER HUNTINGTON'S GIFTS OF LAND
AND GIFTS TO MUSEUMS

ALTHOUGH ARCHER HUNTINGTON preferred anonymity it was known that he was a benefactor to many institutions. The following two lists found among the Huntington Papers in the collection at the Syracuse University Bird Library attest to this.

The first is a transcription of a handwritten sheet in the collection; the second was from a black three-ring binder in the collection titled Volume 139 Gifts and Endowments. There is no suggestion that these are complete lists of Archer Huntington's gifts.

VOLUME 139 (YELLOW) GIFTS TO MUSEUMS: LIBRARY AND COLLECTIONS

Academy of Arts and Letters (Mus. of the)
Brookgreen Gardens
Bryn Mawr College
Casa de Cervantes
Charleston (Gibbes)
Charleston Museum
Church of Our Lady of Guadaloupe
Church of the Lakes—
City of New York (Museum of)
Ciudad Universitaria
Design (Nat. Acad. of)
Fogg Art Museum
Geographical Society (The Amer.)
Golf Museum
Greco (Casa de)

Henry Edwards Huntington Library and Art
  Collections
Hispanic Society of America (The)
Historical Society (The New-York)
Hospital (The General Memorial)
Huntington Free Library and Reading Room
Indian (Museum of the American) H.F.
Institute of Arts and Letters (National)
Kenyon College
Library of Congress
London Library
London University
Mariners' Museum
Metropolitan Museum of Art
Mike de Young Museum

Natural History (Amer. Mus of)
Newcomb (Town of)
Numismatic Society (The Amer.)
Palace of the Legion of Honor
San Diego (Mus. of)
Sculpture Society, National
Sevilla Art Sevilla (Archaeological)

Smith College
Syracuse University
Texas University
Ticonderoga Mus.
Wellesley College
Yale University

VOLUME 139 GIFTS OF LAND AND ENDOWMENTS IN HUNTINGTON COLLECTION

American Academy of Arts and Letters
American Geographical Society
American Numismatic Society
Brookgreen Gardens
Church of Our Lady of Guadeloupe in New York City
Church of the Lakes in Long Lake, NY
Heye American Indian Museum
Hispanic Society of America
Huntington Free Library in Bronx, NY

Henry Edwards Huntington Library, Art
  Collections and Botanical Gardens
Mariners' Museum
Newcomb, NY
State of Connecticut
State University of New York
Syracuse University
University of Texas in Galveston, TX

VISITS TO BROOKGREEN AND OTHER TRAVEL
AS DATED IN ANNA'S DIARIES

October 6–10, 1929—Roundtrip from New York to look at the Four Colonial Plantations, Georgetown, South Carolina

January 2, 1930—Depart from New York for Brookgreen. (Jan. 24, 1930—Archer buys Brookgreen for $225,000). Cruise on the *Queen Anne* to Haiti, Havana and Santiago in Cuba

May 4, 1930—Return to New York

January 1931—Depart from New York. (no date)

May 15, 1931—Return to New York

Dec. 1, 1931—Depart from New York

June 1, 1932—Return to New York

August 3, 1932—Depart from New York for Leysin, Switzerland

September 15, 1933—Leave Switzerland for Lago Maggiore, Italy

October 14, 1933—Return to Rocas (Haverstraw, New York)

November 27, 1933—Depart from Rocas for Tucson, Arizona

March 15, 1934—Depart from Tucson, driving through San Antonio, Texas, Louisiana, Savannah, Georgia, to Brookgreen

March 20, 1934—Arrive at Brookgreen

May 7, 1934—Return to New York and Rocas

December 19, 1934—Depart from Rocas

May 8, 1935—Return to Rocas

December 19, 1935—Depart from Rocas

April 10, 1936—Return to Rocas

December 21, 1936—Depart from Rocas

March 14–21, 1937—Florida

May 12–21, 1937—Lexington, Kentucky, to Kanawha River, Roanoke, Virginia, and return to Brookgreen

May 31, 1937—Return to Rocas

December 18, 1937—Depart from Rocas

April 1938 (no date)—Return to Rocas

December 20, 1938—Depart from Rocas

April 3, 1939—Return to Rocas

March 13, 1941—Depart from Stanerigg

April 6, 1941—Return to Stanerigg

January 3, 1946—Depart from Stanerigg

April 3, 1946—Return to Stanerigg (Last visit to Brookgreen)

BIBLIOGRAPHY

Adelson, Howard L. *The American Numismatic Society 1858–1958*. New York: The American Numismatic Society, 1958.

American Kennel Gazette: "Stanerigg's Aid Renews Scottish Deerhound Fever in United States." Arthur Frederick Jones, 1939.

——. "Stanerigg's Modern Kennels Supplement Charm of Legendary Scottish Deerhound." Arthur Frederick Jones. 1940. Published Material, Series IV, Box 5, *Anna Hyatt Huntington Papers*. Syracuse University Library Special Collections.

Auchincloss, Louis. *The Vanderbilt Era: Profiles of a Gilded Age*. New York: Charles Scribner's Sons, 1989.

Bailey, Anthony. *Rembrandt's House*. Houghton, Mifflin Co. Boston, 1978.

Brookgreen Journal, Vol. XX, No.1. 1990. Editor: Robin R. Salmon. *The Huntingtons: Twentieth Century Visionaries*. Excellent, informative article about the Huntingtons at Brookgreen Gardens. No byline. 6 illustrations. End-notes.

Claim-Stefanelli, Vladimir. *The History of National Numismatic Collections*. Washington, D.C.: U.S. Government Printing Office, 1970.

Contini, Cesare. Interview, August 28, 1978. by George Gurney. *Archives of American Art*, Smithsonian Institution, Washington, D.C. Microfilm 3612.

Cook, Doris E. *Woman Sculptor: Anna Hyatt Huntington (1876–1973)*. Prepared with the support of the Connecticut Commission on the Arts through the Connecticut Foundation for the Arts. Hartford: October 1976.

Croffut, W. A. *The Vanderbilts: The Story of Their Fortune*. Chicago and New York: Belford, Clarke and Company, 1886. Appendix E, 305. It is part of a series called *The Leisure Class of America*. Published by the Arno Press, New York: New York Times Company, 1975. This book contains the full text of William H. Vanderbilt's will.

Dearinger, David B. "Anna Hyatt Vaughn Huntington (10 Mar., 1876–4 Oct. 1973)." *American National Biography*, v.11. New York, Oxford University Press, 1999. 527–529.

——. *The Archer M. Huntington House at 1083 Fifth Avenue*. New York, The National Academy of Design. 2002.

Dickinson, Donald C. *Henry Huntington's Library of Libraries*. Huntington Library Press, 1995. 84.

Directory of American Scholars. 7th ed. (v. 3) New York & London: R. R. Bowker Co. 1978. "Jose Garcia-Mazas."

Edwards, Susan Harris. *Anna Hyatt Huntington, Sculptor and Patron of American Idealism*. Submitted in partial fulfillment of the requirements for the

Degree of Master of Arts in the Department of Art, University of South Carolina. 1983.

Evans, Cerinda W. *Collis P. Huntington, Biography*. 2 vol. Newport News, Virginia: Mariners' Museum, 1954.

———. *Anna Hyatt Huntington*. The Mariners' Museum. Newport News, Virginia. 1965.

Gienapp, William E. *Abraham Lincoln and Civil War America*. A Biography. Oxford University Press. 2002.

History of the Hispanic Society of America. Written by members of the staff. New York: Hispanic Society of America, 1954. Published to celebrate the Fiftieth Anniversary of the Hispanic Society of America. Archer M. Huntington was president of the H.S.A. from its inception in 1904 to its Fiftieth Anniversary. He was behind almost every initiative the staff took and guided them personally throughout this fifty-year period. Yet he did not want his name mentioned except in the introductory pages. He was, essentially, a deeply modest man.

Hoffman, Ellen S. *Columbus' SPAIN*. Washington, D.C.: TimeTraveler, Inc., 1992.

Huntington Collection: *Anna Hyatt Huntington Papers*. 27 boxes, 4 oversize packages (34 linear feet). Syracuse University Library, Department of Special Collections, 600 E. S. Bird Library. Syracuse, New York. In her will, executed after her death in 1973, Mrs. Huntington left all her papers of a "biographical nature" to Syracuse University.

———. *Archer Milton Huntington Papers*: Selected Correspondents.

———. *Archer Milton Huntington Estate Papers*.

Lavender, David. *The Great Persuader: The Biography of Collis P. Huntington*. P.O. Box 849, Niwot, Colorado: University Press of Colorado, 1969.

Masters, Raymond D. *The Huntington Wild Life Forest: A Social History*. Utica: North Country Books, Inc. Publisher-Distributor, 1993.

Maher, James T. *Twilight of Splendor*. Boston and Toronto: Little, Brown & Co., 1975. This book includes a definitive summary of the life of Arabella Duval Huntington before and after the birth of Archer M. Huntington. It is based on the thorough research by Cerinda W. Evans, Librarian, Mariners' Museum, Newport News, Virginia. Miss Evans's monograph was published after the death of Archer M. Huntington, Dec. 11, 1955. It does not circulate.

Matt, Fletcher. *Morocco*. 5th ed. Victoria, Australia: Lonely Planet Publications PTY Ltd., 2001.

Mayor, A. Hyatt. *A Century of American Sculpture*. New York: Abbeville Press, 1988. In the *Introduction*, A. Hyatt Mayor, Curator Emeritus of the Metropolitan Museum of Art and Anna's nephew, tells how Collis Potter Huntington and Arabella Duval Yarrington, Archer's mother, met, fell in love, and how she bore his son, Archer. He also tells how Anna and Archer were married. Other sections in the book describe the sculpture collection and how the Gardens were developed. Another chapter by Robin Salmon gives the colonial history of Brookgreen Plantation.

Mayor, Brantz. "Uncle Archer." *Reminiscences* of Archer Huntington and his life with Anna by

Anna's nephew, A. Hyatt Mayor's younger brother. He spoke at a memorial gathering after Archer's death at the Library of Congress, Washington, D.C. A copy of this essay is in the Huntington File at the Mark Twain Library, Redding, Connecticut.

Mazas, José García-. *El Poeta y La Escultora*. New York: Hispanic Society of America, 1962. Written in Spanish. Printed in Madrid. 525 pages.

Michener, James A. *Iberia*: Spanish Travels and Reflections. New York: Random House, 1968.

Miles, George Carpenter. *The Coinage of the Visigoths of Spain, Leovigild to Achila II.* Published in cooperation with the Hispanic Society of America and the American Numismatic Society. New York, 1952.

Morris, Lloyd. *Incredible New York: High Life and Low Life of the Last Hundred Years.* New York: Random House, 1951.

New York Times. Obituary, "Archer Milton Huntington," December 12, 1955.

——. Obituary, "Anna Hyatt Huntington," October 4, 1973.

Nye, Frank W. *The History of Redding, Connecticut.* www.historyofredding.com/HRhuntingtonpark. htm. n.d.

Peterkin, Genevieve C. and William P. Baldwin. *Heaven is a Beautiful Place: A Memoir of the South Carolina Coast.* Columbia, South Carolina. University of South Carolina Press, 2000.

Porter, Darwin & Danforth Prince. *Frommer's Spain 2002.* New York: Hungry Minds, Inc., 2002.

Proske, Beatrice Gilman. *Archer Milton Huntington.* Printed by order of the Trustees of the Hispanic Society of America. New York, 1963.

Records of the Probate Court, Town of Redding, Connecticut. Vol. 48, pp. 139–151, for trusts established between 1930 and 1953 by Archer M. Huntington.

Records of the Probate Court, Town of Redding, Connecticut. *Will and Estate Inventory of Archer M. Huntington.* Vol. 24, pp. 359–360.

Records of the Probate Court, Town of Redding, Connecticut. *Will and Estate Inventory of Anna Hyatt Huntington*, Vol. 39, pp. 840–851. *Codicil*, Vol. 39. pp. 852–854.

Reynolds, Donald Martin. *Masters of American Sculpture: The Figurative Tradition from the American Renaissance to the Millennium.* New York: Abbeville Press, 1993.

Rothman, Sheila M. *Living in the Shadow of Death: Tuberculosis and the Social Experience of Death.* New York: A Division of Harper Collins, Publishers, Inc., 1994.

Schaub-Koch, Émile. *L'œuvres d'Anna Hyatt Huntington.* Edition Mession. Paris. 1949. Written in French. Author was Professor in the Art Department of La Sorbonne. Our copy came originally from the library of Anna Huntington who had received it from M. Schaub-Koch in October 1949.

Stern, Robert A. M. *New York 1930.* New York: Rizzoli International Publications, Inc. 597 Fifth Avenue, New York, N.Y. 1987.

Tazewell, William L. *Newport News Shipbuilding: The First Century*. Newport News, Virginia. The Mariners' Museum, 1986.

Thorpe, James. *Henry Edwards Huntington: A Biography*. Berkeley: University of California Press, 1994. 623 pages. This well indexed book about the founder of The Huntington Library, Art Collections, and Botanical Gardens in San Marino, California, has a tremendous amount of information about his family as well as Archer's, about Arabella, Archer's mother, about her palace at 2 East Fifty-seventh Street, New York, and many references to Archer and Anna Huntington.

Tinker, Edward Larocque. *The Hispanic Society of America: Spanish Art in New York*. New York: 1958. Reprinted by permission from THINK Magazine, copyright 1953 by International Business Machines Corporation. This booklet was found in the *Anna Hyatt Huntington Papers* at the Syracuse University Bird Library, *Published Material, 1958–1960*. Series IV, Box 1.

Visitor's Guide—"Huntington Beach State Park." South Carolina State Park Service, Columbia, South Carolina, 2001. The booklet contains the story of how "Atalaya," the Huntingtons' winter home situated within the State Park boundaries, was built. Archer Huntington was architect. It also has a well-illustrated section on the flora and fauna of the coastal region.

West, Ronda. *On Fifth Avenue Then and Now*. Birch Lane Press. Carol Publishing Group, New York, N.Y., 1992.

Williams, Susan Millar. *The Lives of Julia Peterkin*. Athens & London: The University of Georgia Press, 1997.

Wright, John Kirtland. *Geography in the Making: the American Geographical Society 1851–1951*. New York: The American Geographical Society, 1952.

INDEX

166

Books by

MARY MITCHELL AND
ALBERT GOODRICH

Newtown Trails Book
1991, 1992, 1994, 1997, 2000

Touring Newtown's Past:
The Settlement and Architecture of an
Old Connecticut Town
1996

MARY MITCHELL

A Walk in Georgetown, 1966

Divided Town, 1968

Annapolis Visit, 1969

Washington: A Portrait of a City, 1972

Glimpses of Georgetown, Past and Present, 1983

Chronicles of Georgetown Life 1865–1900
1986

Chronicle of a Marriage
HAS BEEN TYPESET USING JANSON TYPES
AND PRINTED ON MOHAWK SUPERFINE TEXT
AT THE STINEHOUR PRESS, LUNENBURG, VERMONT
IN THE SUMMER OF 2004
BOUND BY ACME BOOKBINDING,
CHARLESTOWN, MASSACHUSETTS

DESIGN BY PAUL HOFFMANN